CU00691258

72
33R

EELS

John Sidley

Beekay Publishers

First published by 1990 by
BEEKAY PUBLISHERS
WITHY POOL, BEDFORD ROAD,
HENLOW CAMP, BEDS. SG16 6EA
© Beekay Publishers 1990
ISBN 0 947674 29 2

Typeset by BP Integraphics Ltd., Bath, Avon
Printed in Great Britain at The Bath Press, Avon

Contents

Photographs by the author and friends

Line drawings by Len Gurd

Front cover: the author with a 6.02 eel

About the Author

Ever since childhood, the freshwater eel, Latin name *Anguilla anguilla* has held a great fascination for me. For as long as I can remember I have fished for eels. After many years of fishing rivers and canals and handling many hundreds of eels, the best weighing in at 5 lb 8 oz from the River Severn at Severn-Stoke, below Worcester, I turned my attentions to stillwaters. After seeing pictures of two very large specimens taken on night lines for pike at Earlswood Lakes in Warwickshire, it was to be at the small lake at Earlswood, known locally as the Private Lake, that I started this new type of eel fishing.

In the years to follow, I have taken many eels of 4 lb or more. In twelve years of keeping records, my tally of eels at February 1990 is 208 over 4 lb. This includes 37 over 5 lb, 12 over 6 lb, 3 over 7 lb and my largest to date at 8 lb 3 oz.

My ambition in eeling is to land an eel weighing into double figures. After twenty five years, I'm still in pursuit of my only dream. Many anglers did not believe that the freshwater eel could or even would grow into double figures, even though in past history books, there had been records of eels reaching weights of over 20 lb! Many anglers did not believe my story of the eel I lost at Earlswood on the same night that I took my 7 lb 1 oz fish. That lost eel made the 7 lb 1 oz eel look like a bootlace. A lot of those anglers had to eat their words when in 1978, Stephen Terry landed a monster weighing in at 11 lb 2 oz from Kingfisher Lake in Hampshire, while carp fishing. At this time I would like to add my sincere congratulations to Stephen for a most outstanding achievement, even though I had mixed feelings when Stephen landed his eel, for as I have already said, it was my ambition to be the first to land a double. Stephen's eel had confirmed what I had said for many years; eels do exist in our waterways well into double figures.

After the capture of Stephen's new record eel, many good eel anglers gave up their pursuit of trying to beat the old record of 8 lb 10 oz. Some even gave up eel fishing altogether. Myself, I'm still trying, but not to crack the record, just that elusive ten pounder. I enjoy my eeling, even if my eels weigh only a few ounces. In trying for a 10 lb eel I have taken some very impressive hauls of eels. In my 1980 eel season fishing Westwood Park, Droitwich, I landed what was thought to be the largest single night's haul of eels. My total was 23 eels for a total weight of 68 lb 6 oz. There was 1 eel over 1 lb, 11 eels over 2 lb, 8 eels over 3 lb, 3 eels over 3 lb 8 oz, 2 eels over 4 lb and 1 eel over 5 lb. I did better than this in my 1988–89 season.

My 1980 season total was also the best ever taken. It consisted of 21 eels over 1 lb, 70 eels over 2 lb, 54 eels over 3 lb, a staggering 15 eels over 4 lb, 2 eels over 5 lb and a best at 7 lb 14 oz. In 1986 I almost repeated this total with 83 eels over 1 lb, 107 eels over 2 lb, 50 eels over 3 lb, 15 eels over 4 lb and 1 over 5 lb with a best at 6 lb 10 oz. In 1987 my total was 53 over 1 lb, 65 over 2 lb, 21 over 3 lb, 13 over 4 lb and 2 over 5 lb, best at 5 lb 7 oz, all from about 125 sessions. In the 1988 season I landed 35 over 1 lb, 64 over 2 lb, 26 over 3 lb, 10 over 4 lb, 3 over 5 lb and 1 at 6.0. Total sessions: 119. In 1989 my total was 40 over 1 lb, 61 over 2 lb, 25 over 3 lb, 8 over 4 lb, 2 over 5 lb, 2 over 6 lb, the best at 6.7. Total sessions: 112.

My other love in angling is for pike. Since 1974, the beginning of my pike career, I have landed well over 1300 double figure fish with more than 72 pike over 20 lb, the best, a River Severn pike of 30 lb 3 oz.

In the following pages of this book, I have put down my methods of success. I hope you find my methods helpful, but most important of all, rewarding to you in the capture of specimen eels. I wish you all good fishing and end by saying

'PLEASE PUT THEM BACK ALIVE'.

I would like to put on record my thanks to many friends who have helped make this book possible. In particular Brian Crawford, Dick Walker, Gerry Rogers, Barrie Rickards and special thanks to Mrs. Susan Lewis for typing out the manuscript. Finally, I should like to thank Kevin Maddocks of Beekay for publishing this book.

John Sidley
'The Eel Ferret'
May 1990

Introduction to the Eel

Anguilla anguilla is more commonly known to most, if not all anglers in Great Britain as the freshwater eel. The distribution of the eel in Great Britain is vast. It would be far easier to name areas where the eel was not present. The eel will be found in all types of water from rivers, brooks, streams, reservoirs, lakes, park pools to farm ponds. In addition, eels have been recorded in lakes which are classed as land-locked, meaning there is no source of supply of water to keep these lakes full, relying on rainfall only. These facts bear out that eels will leave the water of other systems, travelling overland, for it has only been in the latter years that eels have been introduced by man to inland lakes to help in conservation measures.

For the reader who may not be familiar with the freshwater eel I will explain as best I can its distinguishing characteristics and its life cycle. The body of the eel is elongated, reaching lengths of over four feet. Its girth measures into double figures in inches. The mouth of the eel is very well developed, a strong jaw showing characteristics of the snake family. The mouth is fully toothed to help seize its prey, for the eel, like a pike, perch or zander, is a predator feeding on dead and dying fish, worms and snails. The eel is a scavenger in the true sense of the word.

The fins of the eel are all soft-rayed. The dorsal is long, joining with the anal fin and ending at the vent. The scales of the eel are very small and embedded into its body, being invisible to the human eye. There are only two species which need to be separated, the European eel which is a visitor to Great Britain, and the American eel. The difference between the two is the number of vertebrae; *Anguilla anguilla* has between 110 and 119 and the American eel, *Anguilla rostrata*, between 103 and 111.

The life cycle of the eel starts in the Sargasso Sea (20–35 degrees North and 30–70 degrees West). After spawning on the bed of the Sargasso Sea the adult eels are said to die, the larvae of their young floating to the surface and drifting passively towards the European and North American coasts. At this point a decisive role is played by the warm gulf streams, which brings the larvae to our shores. This journey takes three years. When the larvae reach our river estuaries, the sudden contact with freshwater releases the mechanism of metamorphosis which turns the larvae into eel-like creatures. These small eels are called elvers.

The elver at this stage in its life is transparent but pigmentation increases as it moves upstream against the river currents. Still as elvers, many eels remain in the brackish waters of our estuaries, but many millions travel up our rivers. On nights of no moon, coupled with heavy dewfalls or rain, they leave the rivers by means of dykes, ditches, brooks and on occasions moving over wet ground and holding up in small pools or marshland during the daylight hours, beginning their journey again at night, until a home is found in the form of stillwaters.

In freshwater it is mostly the females who head inland and grow to a larger size, the males spending their life near the estuaries and along the coasts. The females will spend some eleven to fifteen years in freshwater, reaching a weight of around one and a half to two pounds.

At this stage in their life, the urge to spawn and return to their birthplace, the Sargasso Sea, takes over. This is classed as a migration run which takes place between March and April, usually to coincide with flood waters on our main rivers. In the estuaries, the mature females are joined by the mature males and they actively swim towards America to complete their life-cycle where it starts and ends. After spawning both sexes die.

The population in Europe depends nowadays on stocking. Where the resistance of eels to pollution and to changes of the rivers are concerned, this species is probably the most insensitive. In fact it can survive almost anywhere. Sadly the eel is exploited by over trapping. There is evidence that catches of young eels, not only in our English rivers but of European rivers (eg., Weser, Elbe, Ems) have declined considerably. Known and recorded massive migrations through our estuaries already belong to the past. It is believed that over-fishing of juvenile eels and pollution of river mouths have contributed to their decline.

Conservation measures are taken to try and regulate catches. These proposals are now under consideration. It is strongly recommended that in certain estuaries young elvers should have free access to and from the higher reaches. Means of allowing them to do so should be by eel passes but either they are not used or are not kept in good order. Other measures should involve a close season on over netting and a higher licence fee for eel trappers; this proposal was put forward by the British Eel Anglers Club in 1981.

Large eels in excess of 2 lb 8 oz or more are classed as barren eels which means that they never get the urge to return to spawn, so live out their life in inland waters. Reports of eels well into double figures being found dead or trapped, some in excess of twenty pounds, can be

'Three steps to heaven'—this fantastic 7 lb 14 oz accompanied 'snakes' of 3 lb 4oz and 4 lb 8 oz one night at Westwood Park.

borne out by the British and World Record of a rod and line caught eel of 11 lb 2 oz, taken by Stephen Terry from Kingfisher Lake in Hampshire.

One important change in the appearance of the eel while in freshwater can be seen by the coarse angler. During its stay in our waterways, the eel's body colour is usually bronze or a light brown with a yellow belly and their eyes are very small. Some eels show the colouring of a light green or even jet black. This colouring of the eel's skin coincides with its environment, ie., green when hiding in green vegetation or weed beds, black when burying itself in silt and mud on the bed of the lake. Some eels are caught with a two-tone colour of green and black. Half the eel has been lying in its chosen cover, the rest being uncovered.

The other change in the eel is when the urge to spawn and to leave the lake takes over. The eyes of the eel will become very enlarged and the colouring of its skin changes almost to a complete silver. These we call 'Going back fish', ie., mature silvers. It will also be noticed that there are no sex organs while the eel is present in freshwater, and no sperm or eggs. The sex organs develop only when the eel reaches salt water. It is presumed that all large eels are female.

The eel by nature moves about mainly at night, for like bats, hedgehogs and owls, it is a nocturnal feeder. The larger specimens are readily caught more during the following conditions:—

Nights of no moon.
Humid with thunder in the air.
The hotter the better for water temperatures.

Yet eels will feed during the daylight. Clear skies with bright sunshine are not looked upon as ideal eel conditions, whereas the days of overcast skies and foul, dirty weather conditions being classed best.

The eel is also a warm water fish, preferring water temperatures from forty-nine degrees Fahrenheit to well up in the seventies. It is between the months of May and August when the eel is more active. When the Autumn arrives and water temperatures start to drop, the eel's freedom to go in search of food declines. As the frosts of winter arrive and the water temperatures begin to plummet below forty-nine degrees Fahrenheit, the eel will go into a state of hibernation. It achieves this by burying its body in rotting weed growth or heavy silt or mud on the bottom of the lake, leaving only the head visible. This allows it to feed on any tit-bits which may come within its grasp. It is rare for eels to be taken by rod and line in winter months unless a long period of mild weather conditions prevail.

The most productive waters to fish for eels in winter are our main rivers. Heavy flood waters running the river in winter-time disturb the eel from its winter home.

The eel's eyesight is said to be very poor, even in clear water conditions, yet the eel has no problem in finding food. Vibrations picked up by the eel's long lateral line on its body, plus its eyesight help a good deal. However, the highly effective smelling out of its food at distances of well over two hundred yards is the main aid in searching for food. It is said that the eel finds and feeds 98% by smell.

To most anglers an eel is an eel, but to the angler who sets his stall out to capture these power packed fighters, certain profiles of the eel can help him a great deal. To explain, even though there is only one species of eel, ie., *Anguilla anguilla* to be found in Great Britain, two different types of eels abound in our waters. The difference shows in appearance only, this difference being in the shape and form of the eel's head, mouth and front teeth. In one type of eel the head is very broad, the mouth very large and their teeth very impressive. On inspection, the teeth of these eels look more like a junior hacksaw blade. This variety of eel we class as a 'predatory' type. Apart from accepting the usual small fry, worms, snails, maggots, slugs, fish eggs and all the other forms of insect life, this eel will readily accept dead fish of over 8 oz. Some of these eels are taken on live and dead fish of over 12 oz.

Reports have been made of these large-mouth type eels regurgitating small frogs and baby birds while being unhooked and some eels have been found dead with small baby wildfowl such as coots, moorhens and ducklings that they have choked on.

On the other scale we have the type of eel whose appearance is exactly the opposite. These we class as worm feeders, meaning they will be caught on all types of baits but very rarely, if at all, caught on large deadbaits, ie., over 4 oz. The head is very narrow and the mouth small and pointed and their teeth can be barely seen. If felt with one's finger by rubbing it inside their mouth, the teeth feel more like very smooth sandpaper.

We are told that evolution takes many thousands of years yet in all the venues I and other anglers have fished, one always finds that the venue holds 95% of one type and 5% of the other. The only place one seems to find 50% of both types of eel is in our rivers. The question that many of us ask ourselves is, 'Do the eels enter each given water as the large-mouthed variety or as the small-mouthed type?' If the answer is 'Yes they do enter our still waters as both types', then why do we find 95% of one and 5% of the other? Yet as I've stated, evolution, we are told, takes many years. So do these eels change their appearance after entering a chosen still water? If this is so, then the theory of evolution is pushed out of the window. I only wish I could give an answer to these questions but I cannot.

These different appearances help the eel angler a great deal in his quest for landing more fish. On fishing a new water and a landing a few eels, say around a dozen fish, the angler can build up a picture of which type of bait can be best used to his advantage. If most eels taken prove to be the large-mouthed type, the use of dead baits will bring more eels. If they prove to be the small pointed-mouthed type, then the use of small baits, ie., lobworms, maggots, brandlings and dead baits under 4 oz will be more productive.

With the large-mouthed variety of eel, regardless of bait used, these fish will fall to the angler's rods, but I am totally convinced that the small-mouthed type eel, regardless of its weight, be it one pound or eight pounds, will bypass a large dead bait showing no interest at all. Yet if a bait like a lobworm or a small fish had been present, the eel would have eaten the angler's offering. I have proven to myself that this does happen. Whilst fishing Westwood Park I have taken some very large eels of four and five pounds in weight, which are the small-mouthed variety. On rare occasions when the eels have fed fast and furious while fishing lobworms, I changed my bait to a dead fish. The result was a blank. I changed back over to a lobworm offering and the action started again. At Westwood in 1980 only six runs came to my rods while using dead baits. All these fish were over the three pound plus mark, the best being 5 lb 11 oz. That was out of a total of 163 fish taken by myself. The figures show 157 eels fell to lobworms.

Yet on putting these points and figures forward on every venue I have fished, one or two rods arc always fished with a dead bait or lobworm regardless of variety found to be present. For who can tell what lurks in the depths of your chosen venue? A venue which produces 95% of dead bait feeders could hold that elusive one monster that feeds only on small offerings, and vice versa.

Location

Locating a water which holds a head of eels is no problem, be it a river or stillwater. It would be far easier to state where eels were not present. The only problem facing the angler is, does the water he has chosen hold specimens? In most cases the only way to find this information out is by the angler fishing the water himself, or alternatively if you are lucky enough to get genuine information off the local anglers who fish the water. Even then the stories of eels over five pounds being taken can and do turn out to be just stories. If photographs can be produced then a true picture can be built up of the water's potential. A write-up in the national angling press accompanied by a photograph is another aid to finding out the water's eel stocks. Failing all the above mentioned it is then left up to you. If the angler has up-to-date knowledge of the eel's life cycle and its feeding habits, then he is halfway home.

Sadly for the eel angler, his species cannot be stalked in the same way as anglers do for carp, tench, bream and even pike, for the eel is rarely, if at all, seen during the hours of daylight and near on impossible to be seen in the dark. It is no good climbing a tree in the hope of seeing an eel swimming by or feeding on the edge of a weed bed or gravel bar. The only times an eel will usually be seen by an angler is when the fish is in distress or dead or after being hooked.

On my first visit to a new stillwater I visit the venue when it is in its full bloom of summer growth. This enables me to locate all the weedbeds. The weeds are the ideal hiding place for eels and the food life available in the weeds is in abundance. It is found in the form of snails, leeches, redworm and fish fry. The weeds are also the spawning grounds of the resident bream, tench and roach and when these species shoal up for the ritual of spawning, eels will not be far away, awaiting their feast by feeding on the eggs of the spawning fish. The weeds will also hold dead or dying fish which finally sink to the bottom, and dead animal life such as small birds and hedgehogs, a good food source for the eel.

The eel is a fish that is very quick to learn where food is available. Sudden or slow changes in the contours of the lake bottom, like shallows of two feet deep, dropping away to deeper water are the feeding routes of the eel. The change in water depth will draw shoals of small fish, which in turn attracts any eel in the area. The deep waters in the channels are also first class hides for the eel in the daylight, whilst awaiting night-fall.

Old fallen trees that lie in the lake are good hiding places and the trees attract, once again, small fish and other water life. Old sluice gates on your lake will make a perfect home for an eel. Most sluice gates are very old; the brickwork at the bottom breaks away, and the eel will hide inside the holes left. The green slime which grows on the brickwork, and on the fallen trees, is part of the food supply the small fish feed on. In turn the eels feed on the fish. Near islands on a lake are also feeding and holding places for eels.

Trees blowing in the wind shed their insect life, small fish feeding on the supply of free food. The tree roots which can also be exposed under the water surface will supply an eel with a perfect home. A bank exposed to the wind for most months of the year becomes undercut, again a perfect home for an eel.

Wind direction on the lake should be taken note of for the wind blowing into one bank for most of the season will bring with it dead or injured fish, plus any other form of dead animal life. These areas become hot-spots, the larder for a feeding eel. Isolated bays also become gathering areas for small fish, and the areas where local anglers fish a lot. The bait being put into the water attracts small fish, and once again the eel will follow to reap the harvest.

In my search for the eel you will note that I look for areas that will attract and hold eels. I look for some of the worst swims I can find, for I treat the freshwater eel like sea anglers treat the conger eel. They go in search of old shipwrecks or an area where the bed of the sea is covered in rocks or debris, for this is the home of the conger eel. So why not take a leaf out of their book and adopt the same approach? On rivers, eels can be caught in all types of water conditions, be they slow or fast, deep or shallow, weed cover or no weed cover. Yet certain areas are more productive than others. The areas that I find to be best are in back-swims, either caused by an obstruction in the river by a fallen tree, change in depth or a bank cut out by flood water, causing the flow of the river to be pushed to one side, leaving an area of dead water, e.g., lock cuttings above and below a weir.

Consider islands that are found in certain parts of rivers. On one side of the island is guaranteed to be a deep channel, cut out by a man or by the river currents. These channels, shelving up to the island, are first class feeding areas for the eel stocks.

The pools below weirs are all very good. Many rocks and obstructions can be found. Dead fish are kept in the back-swims below the weirs,

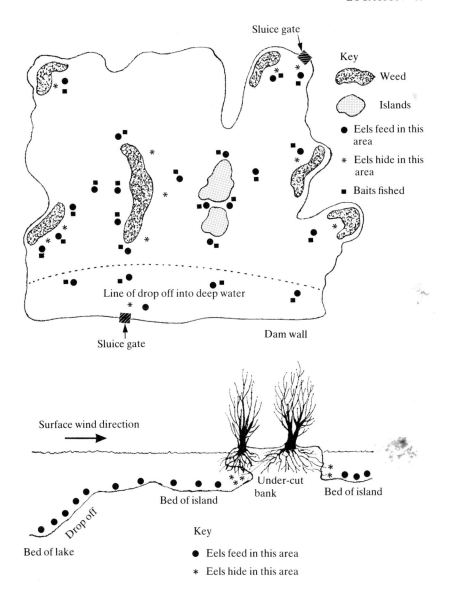

Locating eels near islands

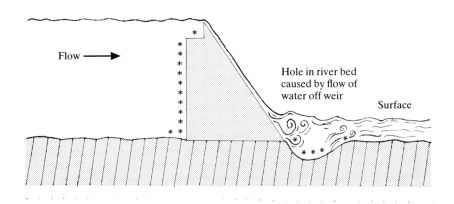

* Eels feed in this area   Weir and weir pool.

Flow ⟶

Hole in river bed
caused by flow of
water off weir

Surface

finally sinking to the bottom. Some weir pools have deep holes, one I know having a depth of over 20 feet; once again perfect holding spots. The areas mentioned above are very good 'hot spots' and worth the eel angler's attention.

On park pools the angler should look for islands or bridges. If your lake should be featureless, the actual margins of the pool are your best bet, as most of the pools are of concrete banks or covered in tarmac. After a heavy fall of rain, any worms or slugs usually find themselves falling into the lake. The resident eels will often hole up in the middle of the lake, or in a deep hole, during the hours of daylight, moving close into the margins at nightfall, to pick up the worms and slugs.

On some occasions, small mud bubbles can be seen coming to the surface, which is a dead giveaway of either a tench, carp, bream or eel sifting about in the mud. A bait placed near these bubbles can result in a fish. Where islands are present, a bait should be cast as close as possible to its banks. On bridges, try a bait dragged down alongside its brickwork. If rowing boats are stored on the lake and left out at night then baits can be cast by the side of them. The underside of these boats seem to attract many small fish.

Once again note the wind direction on the pool. Search for areas which hold dead fish or an area which always abounds with fry. Location on canal systems you may think is impossible, for most if not all are long, straight and featureless. Yet the margins, as found on park pools, are first class. Where there are long bends on the canal, try fishing the far banks of these bends, most of which are tree-lined. On some canals, like the Grand Union and the Stratford Canal, old waterway barges lie rotting away at the side of the canal—the perfect feeding area and home of the canal eel.

Think back to the conger fishermen and their search for old shipwrecks. Disused dry docks used for boat repairs years ago, again holding places, road bridges, old lock gates and the entrances to long dark tunnels. As with lakes and pools, canals have areas where large shoals of small fry gather, also some areas of the canal holding lengths of margin weeds—all these features spell 'eels'.

Try an area fished regularly by the locals or matchmen. The bait put in by these anglers will in time attract shoals of fish, resulting in certain areas of the canal holding a larger fish food supply and it will not be long before the eels take up residence in the area, all this making the location of the eel that much easier.

A fish-eating bird, which is a most vital clue for the angler in his search for areas that hold small fish, especially on big lakes and large reservoirs that are featureless, is the diving bird the great crested grebe. Note the areas where this fish-eating bird dives. In time a picture can be put together on the area which it visits often but make sure that when the crested grebe surfaces he has a small fish in his mouth. If its continuous diving in one spot produces small fish, you can be sure that it has pinpointed an area of small fry. Do not be fooled by a grebe diving in one area and coming to the surface without any fish in its mouth and thinking it has swallowed the fish before surfacing. A grebe must come to the surface to swallow its catch. All of the above mentioned locations and the pinpointing of the crested grebe have, at some time or another, produced eels to my rods. It is worth noting that all the suggested locations should be fished, if possible, day and night. The rest of the work, mainly hooking the eel, is entirely up to you.

Over the many years that I have been fishing for the eel, I have taken note of certain details when I have landed especially large eels. What I have found could be very rewarding to you on your chosen venues. When I fished the lower reaches of the River Severn and Avon many years ago, I did not take much notice of the large eels I took—only the time, bait and swim—yet when I started to eel fish on stillwaters, I found out that on nearly all of my venues, one bank of the lake would be more productive than any other. I was helped in my findings by fellow eel anglers, fishing all banks on my venue. I also found out that the features found on my venues made no odds. On two pits I fished in the Birmingham area it was the banks which were barren of any sort of cover that produced the big eels, yet other parts of the venue really looked the perfect home and feeding grounds for the eel.

For example, at Westwood Park it was the dam wall area of the lake which produced the largest eels taken from that water. The dam wall had a depth of around eleven feet with a layer of thin silt on the bed. There were no weeds or any sudden drop-offs into deep water. The fry shoals on the dam area were no heavier than any other part of the lake, yet those big eels were taken from the dam wall; other banks were covered in heavy weeds, areas of fallen trees, the perfect home for a big old eel, and food in abundance. There were eels taken from these other banks, as anglers were allowed out on boats, but the size of them were very small compared to the dam wall; all eels from five pounds upwards, came from this area—why?

Way back in 1976, I did a lot of eel fishing on the Great Ouse River in Northampton. Once again I found that it was the bank from which I was fishing to be the most productive. The far bank and centre of the river were given fair trial, but it proved in vain. The same thing took place when I eel fished the Worcester and Grand Union Canals. At most times four rods were fished. All had different baits and were fished in different areas, but those big eels only came from one bank.

In another lake I have fished, every eel taken has come from one bank only. The size of the water is forty acres. On this occasion the bank that I have fished and taken all my eels from looks the 'eeliest'. Heavy weed beds, shallow water with odd gravel bars, and the odd fallen tree lying in the lake, the perfect home for any eel. As I have already said, my findings were made a lot easier by having some very keen eel angling friends, who stuck it out on those other banks, regardless of the very many blanks, which were now mounting up. (A way of life for the big eel angler.) It was either from my success or theirs that I started to put two and two together, i.e. six: it was either their bank or mine which was producing the goods. This happened on so many of our venues that it was too much of a coincidence; there had to be an answer.

Not being one to let things lie concerning my eel fishing I got in touch with a fishery biologist that I knew on the Severn Trent Water Authority. I put all my findings to him, and within a few weeks I received my answer. In the Severn Trent netting operations on many of their rivers, canals and lakes, they too had found out that it was one bank only on some of their venues that not only produced the most eels, but some banks only ever produced the biggest. Where eel traps had been set on their venues, some were recovered empty, whilst another set of traps on another bank was removed full of eels. Whilst reading through books regarding eels. I came across a statement made by a Mr. Raymond Perrett in his book called 'EELS—HOW TO CATCH THEM', published in 1958. I quote from page 50...

'Eels have a habit of running along only one bank, a fact proven by the Ministry experts who were demonstrating just what the Dutch fyke nets for eel fishing could do. Nets were set overnight and when removed the next morning (an equal number of nets were laid out on each bank), it was found that the nets on only one bank contained eels—the others were empty.'

So now it seems a proven fact, from my own findings and that of the Severn Trent, plus the netsmen of the Dutch, that on some of our venues, eels will run and feed on only one of our banks, regardless of the features found. If you find the above to happen on your venue, then take heed, get off your backsides and get those rigs into the areas where it matters. On some of the waters where I have eel fished, if the head of eels is very large and their size small, the above mentioned does not always apply, yet on those venues where the eel population is very thin on the ground, but their size very large, do take note of the bank they have been taken from. If the bank you are fishing is producing a big nil, then get over to the other bank fast.

The only form of eeling I have not explored in any great detail, only on location, is river eeling. I have described the areas and what I would class as 'hot-spots'. On our rivers all the eel rigs and bait set-ups mentioned in this book can be put to use in river eeling. The bail arms of your reels can be left in the open position and your main line tucked under an elastic band on your rod handle, to prevent the river current or any rubbish drifting downstream which will result in slack line being pulled from your spool. Whilst fishing an open bail arm, buzzers and all the mentioned bite indicators can be used as well, but my own personal choice lies with my angling companion's (Gerry Rogers) visible bite indicator.

When the main reel line is pulled free from the elastic band and you are not sure if the river current or rubbish is fouling the main line, very gently hold your line between your thumb and forefinger and wait until you feel the slack line being taken up. The pressure felt by your thumb and fore-finger will then tell you if the river current is to blame or if it is indeed a fish accepting your bait. Do not delay the strike when river eeling, for these fish seem capable of swallowing the bait with great speed. When coming to strike your run, wind down as quickly as you possibly can and only strike when you feel, through your rod tip, the movement of the eel. Once again with any new type of fishing, time and practice will make perfect and it will not be long before you can tell the difference between a false run, given by any of the above mentioned, and the true eel taking your bait. As I have said, there is really nothing to mention with regard to river eeling, that is different from stillwater eeling.

When dead-water or backswims are fished, then applying all the still-water methods that I have mentioned will suffice. I must stress once more

6lb 11 oz of pure muscle from Earlswood Lakes on worm.

that river eels do engulf your bait very quickly and seem less worried about line resistance, so wherever possible an instant strike should be made. Any delay in doing so will result in most, if not all, your eels being deep hooked.

There has been a lot of talk and many discussions on the subject of certain swims, on all types of waters fished, and the fact that these areas become unproductive after the angler has removed the first eel or maybe half a dozen eels. My own thoughts on these findings bring me to their 'territorial area', this space of water being a feeding and hiding area. It has also been found that these territorial areas can be of small size, for example a weedbed, a fallen tree, a lock gate or a bridge spanning the water, the same areas in fact that we look for in location.

As the eels in these areas tend to be of specimen size, the smaller eels never appear to be caught. These areas found, the type of bite encountered by the angler is totally different from the usually steady run given by an eel. In fact one would not describe the bite as a run but more of a twitch bite. These twitch bites, I feel resulting from the eel not having to move off with the bait as it is in its own feeding area. If all the above mentioned are found to be true, then this would solve the problem as to why these swims become unproductive. As the angler removes the fish so the swim becomes barren, until a time comes when another eel takes its place.

A typical example of this territorial area was demonstrated to me at Westwood Park Lake in Droitwich. This involved the capture of five large eels. When the lake was opened up to the general public, two local anglers fished a small bay of about 50 yards in size and covered in heavy weedbeds. During a two night stint these lads removed eels of 5 lb 4 oz, 4 lb 13 oz, 4 lb 11 oz, 5 lb 13 oz and a monster of six pounds. The lake has now been open to the angling public for almost four years, yet this bay fished by these lads has yet to produce any eels of the size taken in their first two nights.

It could be said that the eels present at the time in the bay had territorial areas which overlapped each others. The amount of food supply in the bay in the form of snails, leeches, red-worms and fish-fry was plentiful to sustain those five eels. So the question left with the eel angler is, 'Does one stay in one area after a large eel has been taken or move onto new pastures?' My opinion would be to fish the area for at least four stints. If unfruitful by then a move would be my next thought, leaving the area for a couple of months, then returning and trying my luck again.

I must admit that this lack of eels does not happen on all swims. Most, if not all, are productive each season though some do produce blank after blank. Yet a move only some hundred yards or so up the venue will start to produce the goods. So if any of the above happens to you whilst fishing what was a productive swim, do not be afraid to move. I know that it is always in the back of one's mind that when you have moved you could well be missing out on the swim that has produced some big fish, but I believe the move will pay off. It will give time for the area to recover and who knows, if the area attracted eels of the size that the local lads took at Westwood, what size eel or eels will take their place?

I have been asked by many anglers if I could explain why their waters seem to die a complete death, after they have taken a few eels out of their venue, for it is true that once you have hooked and landed a big eel from your water, that eel is never seen again. On a water which is very large, say over 100 acres, it is easy to see why those eels may never be caught. It would be like looking for a needle in a haystack, but this disappearing act also happens on venues which are only a couple of acres in size. It has been said that most, if not all, those big eels hooked, die after being returned, regardless of where the eel has been hooked, i.e. liphooked or guthooked. Their age and the stress of being hooked and dragged out of their environment is all too much. One angler I know liphooked an eel over 6lbs. It fought all the way to the landing net. When netted, the eel was found to be stone dead. A post mortem was carried out on that eel, and it was discovered that the fish had suffered a heart attack. This, I can well believe, for I myself have seen this happen. My good friend Gerry Rogers landed an eel of just 5 pounds from Westwood Park. The hook was in the back of the eel's throat, better out than left in, we thought. I only wish now that I had left that hook in the eel, for as I helped Gerry to remove that hook, the eel's body started to shake violently in my hands. Without warning, the eel's head fell to one side. She was as dead as a doornail. That fish had suffered a heart attack. I have been asked how do I know that I am not catching the same big eels each season, for it is very hard to tag an eel in the same way as anglers tag pike, and one cannot take body marking as in pike fishing, for no pike is identically marked. What I did was to take notes of any marks found on the eel's body, or any deformity the eel had, like only one eye, or a deformed fin or mouth. There were also black or brown spots to be found on the eel's body. These spots grew with the eel. I called them beauty spots. Notes were taken of anything unusual about the eel. If an eel was caught in the same weight bracket, these notes were used to check out the captured fish. As yet, I have only ever caught one big eel twice.

Another way of tagging your eel I was told of by the Severn Trent Water Authority. They advised me to get a pair of very sharp scissors and cut a V in the eel's dorsal fin. They assured me that this would do no harm to the fish, but as yet, I've not practised this method. It is true that those big eels do a 'Houdini' after being captured, so it's back to location for the eel angler. Where do they go? I must agree that some eels do die; as I've seen it happen. Eels returned deep hooked I know do not all die, for I have proven this point many, many times, when I have brought my deep hooked eels home. As I have said on large waters, location is very hard, if not impossible, but on small waters, it should be the law of averages that somebody will hook that eel again. It happens with all other species of fish, regardless whether they are big or small. Even the cunning big carp fall to the anglers' bait in time, but *Anguilla anguilla*—NO WAY.

I have a few thoughts of my own on why we never get repeat captures. One is that those hooked eels may never accept a bait that they have been hooked on before. This was proven when some lads I know eel fished on a local lake. At first, all their eels fell to lobworms. The next season they fished this water, lobworms were not touched. It was deadbaits that scored. The following season lobworms or deadbaits were not touched, it was livebaits that were scoring. This went on season after season, it seemed that the lads had to be one step ahead of those eels on what bait to use. So if your venue has died a death on the baits that you have had past success with, then take a leaf out of my mate's book, and get some new baits flying out into your swims.

You could then start getting amongst the big snakes again. It must be mentioned also, that notes were taken of all eels over 4 pounds, from this water, and those fours did not ever show up again.

What I am going to say now, may sound very far fetched to some anglers, but could those eels hooked on, say, lobworms somehow pass on messages to the other eels in that water, that lobworms are a danger. If yes, this could give the answer as to why lobworms should become unproductive in catching any size eel in that water. As I have said, it's not just the big eels that fail to get caught on lobworms, it's all the eels. The bait is not even touched. We know eels are slow growing fish, so could they have a long memory on what baits are a danger to them; interesting stuff, eh?

My other feelings on this subject, and one I know to be true, is I feel that the eels after being hooked, leave the water, looking for pastures new. To them, that water is a danger. They have been hurt, so pack their bags and look for a safe new home. This was proven to me on two waters that I have fished. The first two seasons the water fished well, it then became harder and harder. No matter how hard I tried, the blanks started to mount up. Any big fish eel angler will tell you the same. The first on a new water will be the one to reap the rewards. The water then becomes harder and harder, to the point where it's not worth eel fishing. On the two waters where the eeling became non-existent, I started to look round the lakes, to see if I could spot any eels at night, leaving the water. What I found on one water had to be seen to be believed. An overflow ran out at one side of this lake. The overflow was made out of 12 inch brick pipe. This pipe went through a small spinney by the side of the lake, and into a tunnel under a main road, which in turn ran into a small stream which went into the River Severn. The tunnel under the road was like a pit, for at both ends the tunnel came up about one foot. When I looked into that tunnel with the aid of a torch, all I could see was a mass of eels swimming around. They were waiting for extra water to come from the lake to lift the height above the pit, so they could carry on their journey down the tunnel to the brook. There were eels from one pound up to fish well over the four pound mark. Those eels were not going back to sea to spawn, they were leaving the lake due to the angling pressure put on by the eel anglers. All told I removed 39 eels from that pit that night and returned them to the lake. If that migration of eels was going on each night of the week, you can well imagine it would not take long for that lake to die a complete death.

There are other lakes near both the lakes which I know the eels to have left. I believe those eels may have taken up residence in those other lakes; all I have to do is find the right one, so next time your lake becomes very hard or dies a complete death and those blanks start to mount up, regardless of baits used, start looking around for a nearby lake. It's all down to location. Believe me, if you find the right location, you will be sitting on a goldmine. Give us a ring if you do!

Tackling Up for Eels

With luck, the main tackle requirements used for the pursuit of eels can be that used by the pike angler. If this species is your quarry you can save the expense of buying new and completely different tackle. The rods I recommend and use are made from fibre glass, a two section rod with a length of eleven feet and a test curve of two and a half pounds with a fast taper action.

The blanks I use are made by North-Western, models 'PK3' and 'PK2' being two piece with a test curve of three pounds, ten feet long and a rod with a fast taper. These rods will cast $1\frac{3}{4}$ ounce leads well over seventy yards using lobworms or deadbait and even specials like meat, cheese etc. Being a fast taper rod, having test curves of two and three quarter pounds and three pounds, they will pick up line fast and most important of all, set the hook home when a run develops. For long range, a lot of power must be put into the rod, pumping out baits some seventy yards or more and fishing maybe into depths of water exceeding eleven feet, taking into account an eel may run well over thirty yards further out into the lake before a strike can be made, and also allowing for the stretch in your main line which I believe can be well in excess of fifteen yards.

The rod needed must have plenty of 'beef' yet at the same time plea-sure can be had while playing a hooked fish. Both the 'PK3' and 'PK2' have the above features. Using these rods at close range only requires the angler to wind down fast and pull into one's run. The need to give powerful strikes is dismissed, the action of the rod will do the work for you. If powerful striking is put into practice at close range the end result will be crack-offs. After a while the angler using his tackle will in practice get to know the limits and limitations that he can put his rods. After a while his methods of striking will become automatic, in fact his own mind and intelligence will tell him when his tackle has reached its limits.

On many occasions I have seen anglers using rods which are too soft for eeling. At night you can hear these lads pumping out baits. The sound from the rod is like a whip-lash. The bait is either cast off or most important, when the bait has managed to be put at the required distance and a run develops, on striking their rods nearly bend double, the strike being put into the bend of the rod. The power should be put at the hook length. All the fish feel is a slight tug and therefore reject the bait and that 'all too often curse' is heard along the bank. 'How the hell did I miss that?'

The rod I went in search for and found, in both the 'PK3' and 'PK2', for my eeling, was one which would do the above mentioned. To put my findings to the test go to your local park and cast a baited rig out across the field. Act as if you were about to cast a bait out across the lake, do not hold back. Put the same effort into your cast as you would whilst fishing a lake. Take a friend with you. After casting out, walk to where your baited hook has landed. With your friend holding the rod ask him to wind down and strike while you hold the hook in your hand. Using these soft rods note the amount of pressure felt at the hook— not enough. It will not even move your finger. The power is lost and the end result is a pricked fish and foul language across the water, plus many rod hours gone to waste.

I wanted a rod that would put the hook into where it matters; the eel's mouth, long range or close range. I also wanted a rod which would not cause me 'crack-offs', yet set the hook and pull my hooked eel from any snags which it may be close to. Let us not forget that a lot of large eels are found to be by weedbeds and under-water snags, and that some eels reach well over three feet long. It is no good setting the hook if the eel can gain line by backing off with its tail, caused only by the excessive bend in your rods. Yet the 'PK3' and 'PK2' did the job, they set the hook. The tip took the full force preventing a 'crack-off' and the rod did not allow the spare line to be given by bending over like a fly rod. Result—the eel was drawn from the snags yet great pleasure was felt through the rods at all times.

Over the years I have tried many brands of line, some cheap, others very expensive and faults were found with all makes. Some were either too supple or too stiff; some stretched too much, others did not, but the main fault was the knot strength, most, if not all, breaking easily. It was not until I was introduced to eleven pound Sylcast that I found a line which came up to my requirements. The stretch was not too great, it was supple to use and most important the knot strength was fantastic and at only £8 or so for a bulk spool of a thousand yards, a line which suits my pocket. Putting this line to the test I found it to break at 14 lbs, on a set of Avon scales and the knot to break at just under twelve pounds. Both these tests were made when the nylon was dry.

In my early days of eeling, line strength was stepped up whilst fishing in snaggy waters, yet today I use only eleven pound Sylcast. The only fault I can find with this line is that on occasions when being snagged up, I have been unable to break the stuff, and have had to cut my line!

A fine example of a 4 lb 11 oz Westwood Park eel taken on three lobworms. Note small, pointed mouth and head.

ind this line to be a very good combination when using rods of a half pounds and three pounds tests and casting heavy weights one and three quarter ounces. It will stand up to almost anything a big eel can put it through. It is also a line I used for all aspects of pike fishing; one could ask no more of a line.

As with all new items of tackle, products improve, and this was to be the case with the main line I used for eel fishing. For years I had stuck to my guns by using and recommending 11 lb (or should I say 14 lb), Sylcast. After tests had been carried out on this line it was found that the 11 lb was in fact wrongly advertised and should have been 14 lb. Not long after the line had been revamped I personally had a lot of problems with Sylcast. It broke easily at the knots and did not seem to stand up to the abuse it used to in past years. With my confidence now gone in this line, I started to look around for a new make. To help me in that search, I had the good fortune to start pike fishing with the lure legend himself, Gord Burton. Gord told me about the main line he had been using for many years. He also informed me that he had done much of his Loch Lomond pike fishing using this line. To me, there was no better advert for a nylon line. The make of my new line is Platil and is made by Leeda Tackle. The breaking strain I now use is 12 lb and I can highly recommend it to any angler who is after big fish of any species. I will not bore you with all the high tech specifications, only to say that the line has yet never let me down and has been helping me land specimen eels and pike along with quite a few other species for many years. The line can be bought on 330 yard spools and costs around £5.00. It is a dear line but I know it is worth paying for the best. This line has all the features of the old Sylcast that I used and if it's good enough for Gord Burton and can take the abuse those Loch Lomond pike can give, then it's good enough for me.

The reels I use are Mitchell 300's, as the deep spools purchased with the reel will hold well over two hundred yards of eleven pound Sylcast. There is not much I can report on the M.300 only that it is a reel I have used for as long as I can remember, my first '300' being the type with the half bail arm. There are many good reels on the market today but old habits die hard and the M.300 has become part of my fishing life. Reels I think should be left the choice of the angler, although the good points of the M.300 are the wide spools, which help a great deal in casting. The retrieve is fast and the push-button quick change spool is a life saver when having to alter one's tackle, especially during the hours of darkness. No nuts to worry about or clutch washers being lost. The clutch of the Mitchell is somewhat poor but most of my line is played off by back-winding and usually only when pike fishing, for to give spare line to any sizeable eel is asking for disaster, especially when fishing near snags, but as I've said before, the choice of reels can be left with the angler. Many makes are on the market so the angler should not be too restricted in choice.

A wire trace is connected to the eye of my hook and connected to my main line via a swivel. I use a wire trace regardless of bait used. (Later in this book I will put forward the points in favour of using wire when eeling.) Attachment of the wire trace to the hook and swivel is quite simple. After passing the wire twice through the eye of my hook and pulling both ends of the wire to make a tight attachment, I then clip on some artery forceps and twist the forceps around the lower piece of trace wire. This done the artery forceps can be removed and then the loose end trimmed off. If required one can cover the ends with Araldite glue for some added protection. I see no need for this however as the wire can be plaited very tightly using the forceps. The type of wire I used to use was eighteen pound Berkley seven stranded. (Due to faults in this wire I now use 15 lb P.D.Q.)

The length of trace is six inches when fishing lobworms, brandlings, maggots, slugs, cheese, and meat, and twelve inches long when using dead fish, whole or sections. My traces are kept on a block of polystyrene, the hook inserted at one end then the wire pulled tight and held fast by a drawing pin at the swivel eye. This stops the wire from being bent and kinked. It also makes for easy storage in one's rucksack. In addition a dozen or so traces can be made up, a task made easy at home. Mistakes could be made on the bank, especially at night.

Other small items include a selection of Mustad hooks (sizes 8, 6, 4 and 2). These being worm hooks number 92641. Live and Deadbait hooks up to size 2. (Partridge Z1).

I have already given my views on the Mustad 92641 worm hooks I use. I feel I should also give you a complete run-down as to why I recommend the Z1 Partridge hooks; as you must agree, hooks are very important items of tackle.

Over the many years that I have been eel fishing, from rivers to canals and stillwaters, I think I have tried every make of hook on the market for fishing livebaits, deadbaits or any other form of fish bait. Some of the hooks used were very poor, others were so bad they are not even worth mentioning. I could never really say to a fellow angler that such and such a hook was the number one for fishing the above fish baits for eels. Well lads, now I can say with my hand on my heart, that the hooks I am now using are, in my view, the perfect fish hook for eels, and the amount of big pike they have helped land, that have nicked my bait at night, go even further to prove how good these hooks really are. I was introduced to these hooks by the Managing Director of Partridge Hooks of Redditch, Alan Bramley. That was over three seasons ago and the amount of eels they have put onto my Avons must now run into the hundreds, with at least five fish over 5 lb and four sixes.

My 27 eel haul in 1988 and my 33 eel haul in 1989 were all landed using Z1 Partridge hooks. I feel these hooks do speak for themselves. The model goes under the title of Partridge Z1 Jack Hilton. They are black and made from high carbon Sheffield steel. The sizes I find ideal are from 2–8 and these will cover all the sizes of livebaits and deadbaits I use. I have found they hold their point for ever, staying sharp regardless of the rough terrain one finds on the bed of many of our gravel pits. The barb on these hooks I find is not too large as is found on many other makes, thus helping you to set the hook with ease, more so when fishing long-range, i.e., 100 yards plus. On other makes of hook that I've used, the point has either bent over or even broken off. Never yet has one of the Z1's ever broken on me, at its point, or at the bend, or at the barb. I know that once I set one of these Z1 hooks into my quarry, that fish will be banked unless yours truly makes a cock-up over it. All in all I cannot praise these hooks enough. They have been a God-send to me in my eeling so I do highly recommend these hooks. Get a few coupled to your wire-traces, for once set, they will land anything that swims.

While I am on the subject of hooks, I would like to make one final mention about the Mustad 92641 worm hooks I use. Over the years these hooks have gained great support from the eel lads, but sadly many lads have found problems in obtaining them. Well I'm happy to report that Mr. Alan Bramley and myself are now in the process of developing such a hook on the same lines as the Z1 but with two slices on the shanks. If you wish further information on the above hooks, then give Alan a ring at Partridge's, their address and phone number is at the rear of the book.

A selection of Arlesey bombs from one ounce to two ounce. Rod rests—the ones that allow line to run free from an open spool while the rods are on their rests. Get one which can be pushed into hard ground and which can be adjusted to different heights (e.g. Peter Drennan's).

Landing nets—should have at least 42 in arms and a net with a depth of four feet or more. The mesh should be of the micro type to prevent any damage to fish caught.

A camera.

A flashgun.

A torch with spare batteries and bulbs.

A towel for washing and drying one's hands after holding your eels whilst unhooking.

A change of clothes in case an uninvited dip in the lake may come your way.

A bottle of headache tablets—there is nothing worse than a bad headache whilst on a fishing trip.

A toilet roll in case one gets caught short!

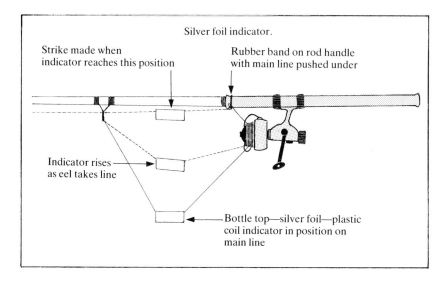

Silver foil indicator.

Strike made when
indicator reaches this position

Rubber band on rod handle
with main line pushed under

Indicator rises
as eel takes line

Bottle top—silver foil—plastic
coil indicator in position on
main line

A supply of plasters in case of cut fingers or hands.

A brolly camp is a must if you are expecting a long session.

A folding chair which can be used as a bed chair for sleeping.

A good supply of hot and cold drinks and food.

Carrying this lot, I must admit, is hard going if a long walk is involved but it is tackle and oddments that can save you time in the long run. For short stints close to access gates, or where the car can be driven to the bank, less tackle is carried.

A most essential part of your tackle is a keep-net or carp sack (such as the KM Safety Sack), if the fish are going to be retained for photographic purposes. The type of keep-net used should be a micromesh and very large, at least eighteen inches wide.

For bite indication there are many suitable buzzers on the market. These include the A.J.S. or Heron. The one I would recommend is the Optonic. This buzzer is a major development in electronic buzzers but other means of bite indicators can be used. A coil of silver paper, a washing-up liquid top, the list is endless. The only fault with an indicator on your main line, which will run free by a taking fish, is the high risk of the indicator twisting on the line and jamming into the butt ring, causing the fish to drop the bait. Further on in this book are drawings of the type of indicator I use and of others used by fellow eel anglers.

One other very important part of one's tackle is a good set of scales; Avon 32 lb × 1 oz are very reliable. They should be kept in the pouch provided and kept clean and dry at all times. If fish are to be kept in your keep-net awaiting photographs or to be witnessed, make sure the net is pegged well out and if possible in deep water. An advantage would be to peg the keep-net in a shaded area away from bright sunshine and any bank noise.

A weigh net, made from micromesh, should be used and soaked in the water before use. Make sure the weigh net is of the large type. The KM Safety Weighsling is ideal as a zip runs along two sides retaining the fish in a completely enclosed bag. Give your captive fish plenty of room to move. Treat all fish regardless of species, with great care and respect and return them wherever possible active and well to the water.

As I have said there are many forms of bite indicators used by the eel angler when legering or free-lining fish baits, worms or specials. Some indicators are better than others but all suiting the individual angler concerned.

The type of indicators that I am talking about are a coil of silver paper, a washing-up liquid bottle top or a plastic wine cap sleeve. Most anglers rely on the modern type buzzers to indicate a run, using no form of visible indicator at all. This is of course one of the most reliable methods, as long as your buzzer does not pack up on the night or day. When the buzzer sounds the angler winds down fast as the eel takes line. When pressure is felt at the rod tip he then strikes. This method I have tried but I feel uneasy using it myself. I like to see a visible indicator rise tight to my butt ring. A few turns of my reel handle, a firm strike, and I should be in contact with my fish. The use of a buzzer and a visible bite indicator can be used as one, the buzzer always acting as the front rod rest. (See drawing.)

Not all eels will pick up your bait and swim off. Some only give slight movements of your main line. These we call 'twitches'. If this was to happen when using a buzzer only it would become quite difficult for the angler to know when to strike. The result could be a deep-hooked fish when the strike is made, or a missed fish altogether. The advantage of any type of indicator placed on the main line, apart from being able to strike when the line can be seen to tighten up, are the indicators that can be seen during the hours of darkness. The wine bottle caps can be obtained in white, the main line can be heard to run through the silver foil and an isotope bobbin can be placed in the bottom of the washing-up bottle top, all giving the angler a better advantage. With all these types of indicators the bail arm of the reel should be left in the open position, so that line can run free. In windy conditions, or with excessive drag on the water, problems arise with the line being pulled from the reel spool. To overcome this in a way which will cause little resistance to a taking fish three devices can perform this function:—

A 4-5 and a 5-2; part of an eleven eel catch from the margins.

This short, fat 6-10 eel was taken on bream head.

An eleven fish catch, including the 4-5 and 5-2, from the margins.

A February eel of 6-2 taken on sandeel following a frosty night.

A daytime catch of six fish included this 4-2 from Barnt Green Reservoir.

A 4-1 and a 3-12 taken just below the surface over 20′ of water one afternoon.

Mick Bowles with an 8 pounder from Weirwood Reservoir.

The reason why a wire trace is essential when using any type of fish bait for eels; this 21-2 pike would almost certainly have bitten through nylon.

A 5-3, two over 4 and one over 3; part of a nine eel catch from the margins on lob worms.

33 eels in one night! This 86-13 record catch represented the largest haul of eels ever caught in one night by one angler.

This 5-03 eel took a fancy to double lobworm about 5′ from the bank.

Needle pushed into ground to allow
plastic coil to rise up to butt rig. When
run or twitch bite develops plastic coil
falls free off main line when rod is
removed from rests.

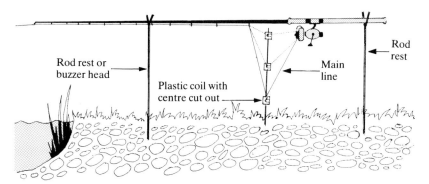

Rod rest or
buzzer head

Rod
rest

Plastic coil with
centre cut out

Main
line

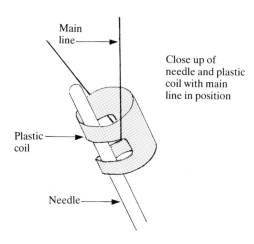

Main
line

Close up of
needle and plastic
coil with main
line in position

Plastic
coil

Needle

Wine cap indicator.

One is an empty line spool container. The line from the reel is placed round the spool on the ground.

The second is an elastic band placed on the butt of the rod above the reel spool. (See drawing.) The line is then tucked under the elastic band. The further the line is pushed under the elastic band will depend solely on the amount of drag one finds on the water.

The last method is a coin placed on the lip of the spool.

All will prevent the line from coming off the spool. Another two methods used for bite indication and for preventing the indicator being blown about by the wind are:—

A needle about 12 inches long is pushed into the ground beneath the reel and at an angle facing upwards to the butt ring. (See drawing.) At this angle no resistance is felt for a taking fish. The indicator is then pulled down over the needle, taking with it the main reel line.

The other method is also using a needle. This time the length of the needle should be able to pass the butt of the rod. The needle is pushed into the ground but instead of being at an angle to the butt ring the needle is positively straight. An indicator of the white plastic coil is used on the main line. Not only is the plastic coil cut up the centre to allow removal but a half moon shape is cut from the centre. The main line then rests on the edge of the half moon cut. (See drawing.)

When a run develops the plastic coil is pulled up the needle as far as the butt of the rod. The upright position of the needle prevents the indicator from twisting on the main line when the rod is removed from its rest. As the indicator rises to the butt, striking at this point allows the indicator to fall free from the main line.

The last types of indicator are the ones which are tied to the back rests. (See drawing.) These can be isotope bobbins protected in a plastic tube with a hairgrip glued to the front, so as to hold the main line in position or the ping-pong ball type. These are painted white or with fluorescent paint. Once again a hairgrip is glued at one end. With these types of indicators, when a run develops the line is pulled free from the hairgrip and the indicators fall back to the rear rests, allowing line to be taken freely. The rod is then picked up and a strike made. On all these bite indicators a front buzzer can be incorporated.

As I have mentioned earlier on in this chapter, there is always one fault or another to be found with these types of indicators. The twisting of the indicator is a bad fault, for we are not always close at hand to our rods, the buzzer failing to go off and the rod with no indicator. Timing the strike is a main fault: too early—a missed fish, too late—a dropped bait. Over the years I have tried all the above types and at

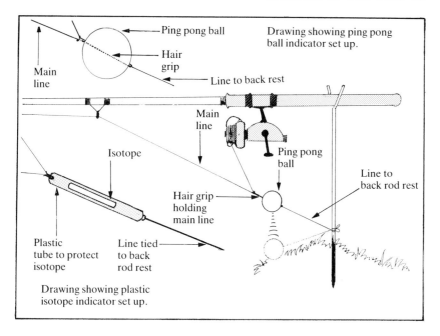

Drawing showing ping pong ball indicator set up.

Drawing showing plastic isotope indicator set up.

one time or another lost fish because of them. It was not until my angling companion, Gerry Rogers, came up with a butt indicator that stopped all the faults found with the other types of indicators. His idea came from the swing tip indicator that is incorporated on the butt of the rod, acting like a swing tip, which is screwed into a top joint, using a terry clip covered in plastic, so as not to damage the rod and one which just fitted the size of our rod butts. Next a small screw was inserted into the bottom of the clip. Over this screw was pushed about four inches of valve rubber, about one eighth of an inch wide. The other end of the valve rubber was pushed onto a sarkanda cane about nine inches long. A gap was left in-between the screw and cane of valve rubber. This gap acted like a hinge to allow the cane to rise and fall. At the end of the cane a short length of gas welding wire was bent round to make a tip ring. Only one of the legs of the ring was whipped onto the cane. The unwhipped leg allowed us to remove the main line from the ring and remove our indicator off the rod, when a long cast was required. Onto the cane was placed a rubber cap of two eighths of an inch wide, just behind the tip ring. After casting out, and the indicator placed in position, the rubber cap was pushed over the unwhipped leg preventing the line from falling out of the ring; the same principal as a necklace clip.

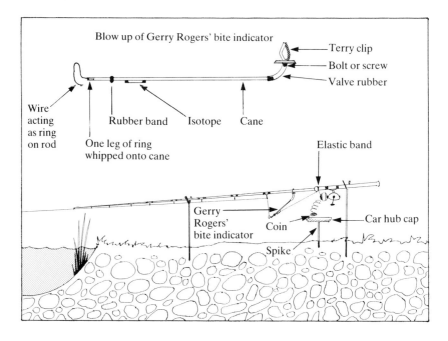

Blow up of Gerry Rogers' bite indicator

Terry clip
Bolt or screw
Valve rubber

Wire acting as ring on rod

Rubber band   Isotope   Cane

One leg of ring whipped onto cane

Elastic band

Gerry Rogers' bite indicator

Coin

Car hub cap

Spike

To aid us in seeing our indicator at night the last four inches of the cane at the tip were painted white and as an added advantage an isotope, protected in a clear rubber sleeve, was whipped onto the cane about 1in behind the ring. The isotope was whipped on underneath the ring to prevent it from hitting the rod when a strike was made. Again this indicator can be used with a buzzer. This may seem very hard to understand but I am sure by looking at the drawings of the indicator you will see how simple it is, so easy to make and all the risks of tangles are prevented.

To put the finishing touches to my bite indicator I incorporate a car hub cap which is positioned under my reel. On my reel spool is placed a coin. When a run develops my indicator rises to the butt and my main line pulls the coin off the reel, which in turn falls into the hub cap making a loud clang. This tells me of a fish taking line. As yet I have never had a tangle using this bite indicator and the hub cap method. I must admit that it may sound crude but it works.

There is one form of bite indicator that I have not gone into and this is the float and float paternoster. The floats were usually used when fishing close range, either in shallow or deep water, by weedbeds or obstructions in the form of sunken trees. The float paternoster was designed to anchor the angler's bait near the weeds or obstructions and

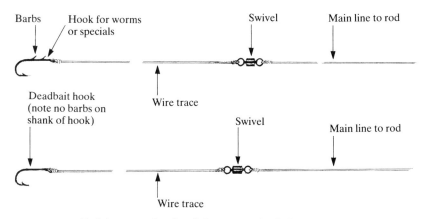

End rig set up when free-lining worms, deadbaits or specials.

in some cases, open clear water.

The paternoster was also designed for days or nights, when wind could cause problems by dragging the float and bait away from the position where the angler so wished it. During daylight fishing, no problem arose for the angler seeing the float, but as darkness fell, the angler was fishing blindly, not knowing when a run would develop.

In the early days of no buzzers to incorporate in the set-up, the only way to overcome this problem was by painting the tops of the floats with fluorescent paint, the only problem being that a torch light had to be shone onto the float and the glow from the float only lasted a few minutes. Now with modern technology, the isotope betalight was introduced into the top of the float. These isotopes can be bought made up, or the angler can buy the isotopes separately and make his own float up to suit different sizes of baits.

These floats are used to carry all types of baits from dead fish to lobworms and specials. In the beginning, the floats were used to present the angler's bait near snag and weeds, as mentioned before. They were also used to present baits on top of the bottom weed. The paternoster rig had to incorporate a lead link weight to keep the bait in one place. The link used was from a low breaking strain line, for the lead was dragged along by a taking fish. If the lead became snagged, the line would break and leave the lead behind. Fishing in depths more than the length of the rod, a sliding float rig must be used, incorporating a stop knot and free running bead. This set-up enabled the angler to fish in any depth found. I must add that the float, these last few seasons, has been used in a way that most eel anglers will find hard to believe or understand. On a week-end fishing stint at Westwood Park, I got talking to a fellow eel angler who had met an ex-member of the National Anguilla Club.

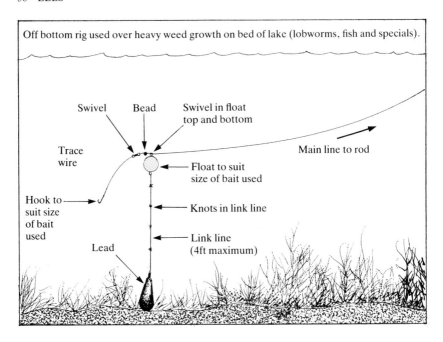

Off bottom rig used over heavy weed growth on bed of lake (lobworms, fish and specials).

During his conversation, varied thoughts and ideas were raised about the feeding habits of the eels. The one most talked about was the reason so many blank sessions were put in by the angler during nights and periods of bright moonlight. A theory was put forward that eels do not go off the feed during these moonlight nights but the moonlight attracted the eels to the surface to feed. Hence this would explain so many blank sessions by the angler, as all our eel fishing is done by legering on the bottom.

Experiments were carried out with both the normal float fished baits and paternostered baits at a well known reservoir in the London area. The baits, regardless of what type was being used, were fished under the surface, even though the average depth of this reservoir was over seven feet. The baits were presented only 1ft below the surface. Their results were most rewarding taking fish in the two to three pound bracket, where anglers normally bottom fishing failed to catch. Since my meeting with this eel angler I have heard of other eel anglers taking eels up to five pounds, fishing one foot deep in twenty feet of water, again on moonlight nights. I must admit that even though I have heard of these methods to have taken fish, and know some of the anglers personally, I have not put this into practice but I thought this method of taking eels should be written into the chapter.

I have described the tackle needed by the eel angler, yet I thought I should leave out the setting up of my end rig and explain in more detail its good points. After my wire trace has been made up to the required length and hook size with the aid of my forceps, my rod is then set up with reel and the line passed through its rings. I then check the first two feet or more of my main line. Any signs of weak spots are then cut off. Having carried this out, my lead weight with a link line connected to an extra large swivel is set up, the link line being at least six inches long. This will prevent my swivel running on my main line from becoming buried in any soft silt or weed, the extra large swivel on the link line helping to stop weed or silt from locking the eye, thus preventing any restrictions to a taking fish. (See drawing.)

The weight used, regardless of distance fished, is $1\frac{1}{2}$ oz, the reason being that if a smaller weight is used, a running fish could easily move or lift the weight off bottom, resulting in resistance. The lead stays in one spot, the main line then running freely through the link swivel. I also find that a $1\frac{1}{2}$ oz, lead balances my tackle out when using 11 ft/10 ft rods with a main line of 11 pounds breaking strain. I think this is a very important point to make, that one's tackle should feel balanced in the angler's hands. If not, one seems to be afraid of putting his tackle to its full use and then mistakes are made. This is very important to all anglers, regardless of the species of fish sought. One must have confidence in the tackle used.

My link line and lead made up are then placed onto my main line. Following this is placed a small running bead and then a small swivel is tied to my main line. The bead acts as a bumper against my link swivel and knot tying the small swivel to my main line. This small swivel acts as a leger stop. With this set-up, long casts can be made without fear of the lead sliding down my main line, as when using split shots. If shots were used or the plastic type of leger stops now on the market, these can so easily pinch one's main line causing a weak spot. Also if these leger stops do slide down and the angler slides them back up his main line, he will notice that his line becomes 'curly'. This has caused a weak spot and on both systems the risk is very high of the angler breaking off at these areas when a strike is made.

The next step in the setting up of my end rig is to tie a piece of my main nylon in between my swivel leger stop and my hook length. This length of line should be around 2 inches longer than the length of my link-leger. This couples up my leger stop to my hook length and at the same time prevents my link line from twisting around my wire trace when casting. If the angler is using a nylon hook length then no problem arises but if a wire hook length is used the link will tangle with the wire. If this was to happen after casting out, when a run developed,

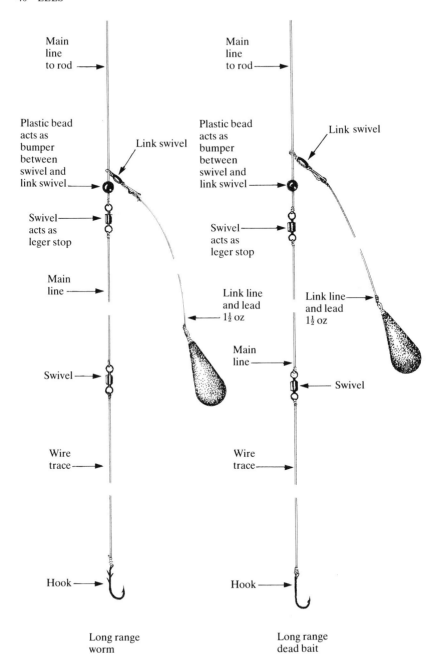

Main
line
to rod →

Main
line
to rod →

Plastic bead
acts as
bumper
between
swivel and
link swivel →

Link swivel

Plastic bead
acts as
bumper
between
swivel and
link swivel →

Link swivel

Swivel →
acts as
leger stop

Swivel →
acts as
leger stop

Main
line →

Link line
and lead
1½ oz →

Link line →
and lead
1½ oz

Main
line →

Swivel →

Swivel

Swivel →

← Swivel

Wire
trace →

Wire
trace →

Hook →

Hook →

Long range
worm

Long range
dead bait

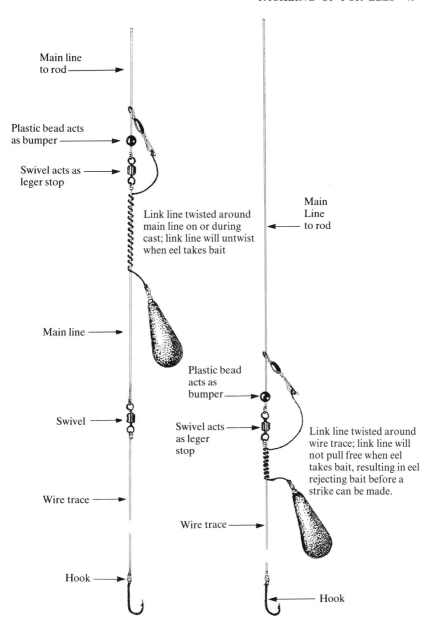

Main line
to rod

Plastic bead acts
as bumper

Swivel acts as
leger stop

Link line twisted around
main line on or during
cast; link line will untwist
when eel takes bait

Main
Line
to rod

Main line

Plastic bead
acts as
bumper

Swivel

Swivel acts
as leger
stop

Link line twisted around
wire trace; link line will
not pull free when eel
takes bait, resulting in eel
rejecting bait before a
strike can be made.

Wire trace

Wire trace

Hook

Hook

the nylon link will not untangle from the wire, causing the taking fish to pull the lead weight as well.

If you find it hard to fully understand the above rigs, then I advise you to set them up in your garden and you will quickly see the above mentioned faults. Instead of using my swivel as a leger stop some anglers use a small bead or section of valve rubber. I have used these two types of methods and have had the main line break, the fault being that the main line is passed through the eye of the bead or valve rubber about three or four times. This in turn holds the leger stops in place on the main line, but where the main line rests on the eye of the bead or opening of the valve rubber, it is prone to becoming weak, caused by the kinking of the line. Also if the line was to lie across itself when passed through the openings it could cut itself in half.

Some anglers that I have talked to, have been put off by the number of knots in my main line in setting up my rig. Their comments are well founded, my end rig does consist of three knots, yet if every knot is checked and all are found to be safe, the angler is only fishing with one knot. That may sound confusing to you but it is only common sense. If all knots are perfect then you only have one knot to worry about. Set my end rig up, fish it and compare it with your own, I am sure you will find it is 100% safe. In all the time I have fished using this rig, and using all types of baits, it has yet to fail me. (This rig is now known in the eel angling world as 'The J. S. Eel Rig'.)

The need to use a trace wire when eel fishing, regardless of what type bait is used, has been an evergreen argument for many years amongst the eel angling fraternity. Some say 'yes, it's needed' others say 'no'. I hope to put forward the many reasons for the need to use a wire trace and hopefully give a fair comment on this, a very much talked about problem. When I first began eel fishing our main rivers, reel lines of up to sixteen pounds were used, yet eels were lost through bite-offs, some biting through the line as if cut by a pair of scissors and others rasping through the line like a file, scouring the line for many inches. At one time I used Dacron backing as a trace material, which is used on fly reels, yet once again bite-offs were the end result. Even some of the large, small mouthed eels on the rivers had teeth which would cause bite-offs. On stillwaters I found the deadbait feeding eels to have even a more set of impressive teeth than their sisters in running water. The problem of the eel's teeth causing break-offs was not only one of the faults in using nylon hook lengths.

Eels are found where there is cover for them to hide. This can be from deep-water holes or obstructions on the lake or riverbed; in weir pools and off dam walls, many large boulders and rocks can be found present. To hook one of these fighters in this terrain on nylon hook lengths is asking for trouble. The fault I think obvious, the nylon hook length, being pulled or rubbed through, these obstructions would part your line. Fishing a wire trace also helps the angler if your hooked eel swims into any reedbeds or bottom weed. Keeping a tight line between you and the hooked fish would cause the wire trace to act like a knife's edge, helping to cut the soft weed.

Some anglers, as I have said before, scorn the use of wire, regardless of baits used. I consider them to be very foolish when fishing any type of fish bait, for the risk involved is very high of an unexpected pike accepting their offering. I am sure that these anglers would not go in pursuit of pike in winter without a wire trace. A 23 lb 3 oz pike from Westwood Park engulfed a small tail section of roach after giving time on the strike for the eel which I thought had taken my bait. When the pike was finally landed, the hook was found to be in the fat of the pike's throat. On inspecting my end rig I found my wire trace to be badly damaged. If I had been using a nylon hook length I would have lost that pike.

Another reason a wire trace is looked down on is the angler's theory that they encounter many dropped runs. I think it is not the fault of using a wire trace, the culprit being small eels unable to get the bait in their mouths, running a few yards then dropping your offering. When an eel capable of taking your bait comes along no problem arises. All the angler encounters is a fulfilled run and a hooked fish.

Another point worth noting, if one sits back and thinks hard about it, is that when an eel picks up a bait, be it worms, fish or specials, its first reaction is to close its jaws tightly round your offering. This action helps to crush your bait, making it easier for the eel to swallow. To my way of thinking, if the eel picks up a worm or four worms and swallows the lot, not taking any notice whatsoever of a size 2 hook, surely a very thin piece of wire is not going to make much difference. I have fished waters using both nylon and wire, day and night, and on occasions having more runs to the rod with a wire trace connection, in fact landing more eels during the fishing period using wire.

On a fishing trip to Westwood Park with *Angling Times*, who were composing a feature on 'Eels and Eel Fishing', Gerry and I decided to use more rods on nylon traces, just in case we found the eels to be finicky over wire. All we wanted was a few small eels to show the paper. At the same time a rod was fished with a wire trace. On that night we took two eels each, the best falling to Gerry at 4 lb 11 oz. Those eels fell to the rods fished with wire traces; the nylon hook rigs never produced a twitch.

I have had it said to me, 'Why fish wire traces on water where 95% of the eel stock is the small mouthed variety with less damaging dental ware?' I agree, but what about the other 5%? What happens if one of those females comes along, or as I have said, the unexpected pike? No,

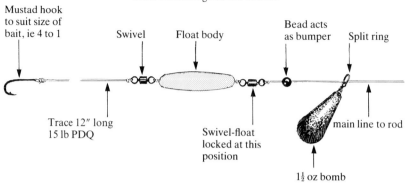

Main line through centre of float

Mustad hook
to suit size of
bait, ie 4 to 1

Swivel

Float body

Bead acts
as bumper

Split ring

Trace 12″ long
15 lb PDQ

Swivel-float
locked at this
position

main line to rod

1½ oz bomb

The JS. off the bottom—mid-water or surface rig (all types of baits can be used).

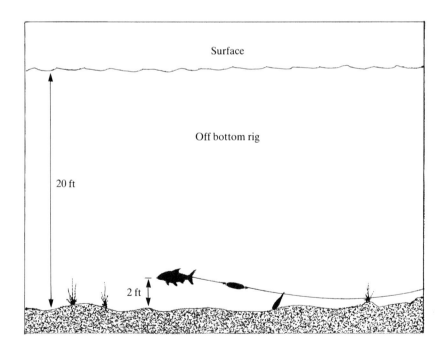

Surface

Off bottom rig

20 ft

2 ft

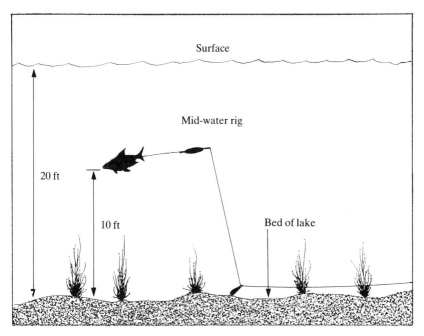

Surface

Mid-water rig

20 ft

10 ft

Bed of lake

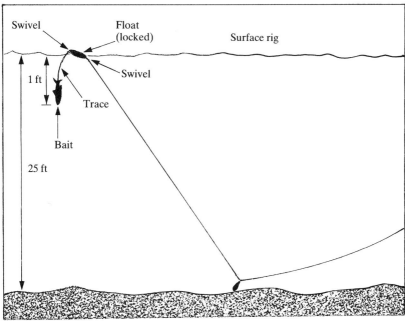

Swivel

Float
(locked)

Surface rig

Swivel

1 ft

Trace

Bait

25 ft

the risk is too high. Let us not forget that an eel is a predator and they have been equipped with the appropriate teeth. If you are still in doubt that wire is not needed then take heed of the angler who confronted me at Westwood Park last season. He told me and other anglers on the bank, that he had never used a wire trace in his whole eeling career and had seen no need to use one. I tried to explain my reasons to him for using a wire trace. My explanations were more or less laughed at. He had landed eels well over five pounds. I walked away and let him get on with it. On that night only two small eels were landed. The angler who had been scorning the use of wire had his first run using lobworms. When a strike was made his rod powered over. This was a good fish. Myself and others walked down to watch the playing and landing of his eel. After a very good fight the eel surfaced some 20 yards out. Seeing the eel for the first time, she looked well over the 4 lb mark, but in the stillness of the early morning, we could hear the sound of the eel's teeth rasping across his nylon as she shook her head from side to side. Seconds later the bend in his rod disappeared and the main line went slack. All that could be seen was the disturbance on the lake's surface and the swirl as the eel disappeared back into the depths. She had bitten him clean through. I shall always remember the look of disbelief on his face. I felt a certain amount of pity for him yet I only spoke once. My comment and the only one suitable at the time was, 'You don't need a wire trace for eels, do you?' There was no reply from him. The following week I saw him again. His rig had changed. A wire trace was now coupled into his rig. You must agree that it was a costly way to find out his mistake.

Over the years I have tried many types of wire, yet I find the best to date being 15 lb P.D.Q. This wire is bronze in colour, seven stranded, quite thin and supple. Wires that should be avoided are the ones covered in a plastic film and the type which require crimping to fix the swivel and hook. The other type of wire is single strand. If this wire becomes kinked on casting or playing an eel, the kinked area will break like cotton. All told, 15 lb P.D.Q. takes some beating. In three years of using the wire I have lost only one eel caused by a bite-off—a good track record indeed. So when asked if I recommend wire for eels my answer is 'yes'. I recommend it on past hard won experiences—but the choice is yours.

In the first edition of my eel book, I wrote about the rods I used whilst eeling. Since then I have been in touch with a certain Paul Boote, who is a rod builder trading under the name of Graham Phillips. It was to Paul that I wrote, asking if he would be interested in a rod I had designed for eel fishing. With great relief he said 'yes'—the first rod company ever to say yes. What I wanted was an 11 ft carbon rod that would cast any type of bait I used for eels, well over the 100 yards mark, and in deep water. It was no good getting a bait out that far, and in such depths, if, when a strike was made, nothing would happen at the hook end. I also wanted a rod which would be kind when fishing at very close range, or under the rod tip. I wanted the rod to set the hook and at the same time pull my eel off any snags. I did not want the rod to bend over like a fly rod; if that did happen, the bend in the rod could give enough slack line for a big eel to get his tail round any nearby snags. I also did not want the rod too stiff and have the risk of a crack-off, if I hit a big snake under the tip—a tall order you must agree. I'm glad to say that after trying a couple of blanks, Paul came up with the ideal tool, an 11 ft carbon with a test of 2 lb 6 oz, a Century blank with a compound taper. The action of the rod went down into the handle. Seven Seymo rings plus a tip ring were put onto the blank. The butt ring, being 20 mm, helped casting by breaking down the coils of line as they left the Mitchell 300's spool. Only seven rings and the tip ring on the rod helped a great deal on cutting down line drag when casting to distances of up to 100 yards. This was no problem using lines of 12 lb coupled with a $1\frac{1}{2}$ oz Arlesey bomb and fish or worm baits. No baits were cast off and when a run did develop, the rod did the work by setting the hook home. The look of the rod is very smart and the ever-so-popular look of an eel rod has gone. You know the sort of thing I mean, a rod as thick as a bean pole which would land any Great White Shark with ease, or on the other hand, a rod which would be suited to match fishing or fly fishing.

Testing the rod with Gord Burton of Loch Lomond fame, he too has agreed it's a first class tool, and one that can be put to medium pike fishing, i.e. plug fishing, spinning, sink and draw deadbaits and lives up to about 10 oz. All in all it is the ideal tool. To prove its worth, I have, during 1985, taken tench to 6 lbs, carp to 20 lbs, bream to 7 lbs, pike to 16 lbs, many eels over 2 and 3 lbs and one of 6 lb 6 oz, all on the John Sidley Eel Rod.

Need I say more? If you would like to know more about this rod, then write to Paul at Graham Phillips, or drop me a line. At long last the eel has now been credited with a first class rod. In my opinion— none too soon.

Don't forget — discarded line kills birds and other wild animals

Baits and their Presentation

As I have specified in the location of eels, it would be far easier for me to name waters where eels are not likely to be found. The same applies to the food that an eel will not accept. There is not much an eel will not take for a meal, be it from the small insect life in one's venue to the carcass of some dead animal.

In my years of unhooking eels I have had them regurgitate egg shells, small fish, sections of small frogs, snails, slugs, leeches, crayfish, mussels, worms, maggots, casters and bread—the list is endless. I have in my photograph album, a picture of a $1\frac{1}{2}$ lb eel trying to swallow a small coot or moorhen; both are dead. The photograph was sent to me by Dr. Barrie Rickards. He found the eel whilst fishing a gravel pit near his home. This only goes to show one example of what an eel will expect and try to eat for a meal.

Most, if not all of my largest eels have fallen to lobworms, mainly because I use and concentrate on lobworms more than dead fish, although both types of bait have been successful. Some very large eels have fallen to carp angler's baits, such as luncheon meat. A fine example of this is Chris Taylor's magnificent eel of 8 lb 9 oz. This eel was caught on luncheon meat whilst Chris was carp fishing Three Gates Pool at Wem in Shropshire. The reason I think these eels fall to the baits of these carp anglers is because of their strong smell. Maybe we eel anglers should take a page, so to speak, out of these carp lad's books and start to fish these highly smelly baits. It would be very interesting to see the results if one rod was fished in this manner. A picture could then be established and the results compared with the standard baits.

As I stated earlier on, there is not much to be said or advice to be given on eel baits, but I have compiled my own list of baits which I know to be proven eel takers, and widely used. I have listed the baits as 'Number 1' being what I consider to be the top bait and so on down the list. Yet I must stress that this list is only my opinion, for some venues can differ quite a lot from others. For example, one stillwater I fish in the Midlands has yet to produce an eel to a deadbait, be it whole or section. The eels taken so far in four seasons have fallen to lobworms, yet deadbaits have been fished on every visit. Yet on the other hand, on a stillwater only a few miles away, deadbaits are highly successful. So you can see it will be up to the angler on the venue to come to the final choice. My list and personal choice are as follows:-

No. 1. Lobworms
No. 2. Freshwater fish baits (tail section being the most productive)
No. 3. Brandlings
No. 4. Luncheon meat
No. 5. Cheese
No. 6. Chicken offal (only if used as part of prebaiting)
No. 7. Maggots, slugs, snails, crayfish
No. 8. Sea fish baits such as sprats, sandeels and sardines

My end rig set up for worms is identical to that which I use for my fish baits, the only difference being the hook. The barb is not removed. If it were removed the worms, slugs, snails or any other type of livebait offering would be able to work themselves off my hook, thereby leaving the angler waiting for a run whilst fishing a baitless hook. You will also notice that on all my worm hooks there are two barbs on the shank. The purpose of these is to help prevent any of my baits from working their way down over the bend of my hook to the point, thus covering up the point and making hook penetration harder when a strike is made. These barbs also prevent my offerings, such as four big lobworms, from being pushed down to the bend of my hook when a long cast is made to reach ranges of sixty yards or more. I must stress that these barbs on the shank are not for hooking the eel in any way, their sole function is to help the above mentioned.

To test my findings, bait up with four lobworms on a size two hook and allow your bait to hang down from the rod, as if you were just about to cast. You will see that the worms will all start to fall down the shank of the hook to the bend. Now try the above rig with the hooks with barbs on the shank. You will see the difference straight away. Failing that, bunch your worms onto your hook, pushing them if you wish above the eye of the hook to help hold them onto the shank. Make a long cast and allow this bait to settle as if you were about to fish then slowly retrieve your tackle and you will see that the bait has been pushed round the bend of the hook, covering the point. Do the same cast with my hooks and repeat the above. You will notice the difference. The hook point is not covered and the worms are still on the shank, all making for a better presentation of bait and most important of all, making for a better hooking penetration, and also aiding the angler in stopping the baits being cast off the hook.

Only one fault will be found with my type of hook. This is where

If you talk softly and handle them gently any eel will behave itself for the camera.

the barbs have been made in the shank by the hook manufacturers. If the angler should bend the shank at these points he will find that the hook will break in two without any effort. This may at first bring concern to the angler, yet I can assure you that in all my time using these types of hooks I have yet to have one break, and to date I have landed a fair few eels up to 8 lb 3 oz, some large tench to 6 lb 12 oz and two very big pike of 22 lb 2 oz and 23 lb 3 oz. One can imagine the fighting power and acrobatic display these pike can give in the summer months, being at their fittest, yet my hooks stood up to all the punishment they could give.

It is rare for the hook to become in a position, while playing an eel, for it to break at these barbs, for a hooked eel is at all times swimming in a backwards motion, therefore the hook will be kept in a straight line. One other good advantage is found with my type of hooks. If an eel is found to have the hook well down the throat and only the shank can be seen, the angler can, with the aid of a pair of forceps, insert them into the eel's mouth, clip them onto the first or second barb on the shank, and apply a downward pressure to the shank with the forceps. This will break the hook ensuring less armoury to be left in the eel.

The idea of using broken pieces of lobworms or brandlings came to me after productive results using sections of dead fish. As with dead-baits, my ideas were first put to the test with the eel in my aquarium at home, with the full fish deadbait being only pierced with a baiting needle (see later). I applied the same principle with my lobworms but instead of using my baiting needle to pierce them, I used the hook which I would use whilst fishing. The lobworm was impaled on my hook three times. This completed, the lobworm was carefully removed from my hook, trying my hardest not to break the worm too much and leaving only the small hook holes. To make my tests more interesting I had starved my eel for almost two weeks, not giving him a scrap of food. The time had come to see if my ideas would work. The eel was lying buried in the gravel at the bottom of the tank. All one could see was his nose sticking out about $\frac{1}{4}$ inch. I deposited the pierced lobworm into the tank at the far end. A small amount of greasy liquid appeared on the surface of the water where I dropped the lobworm, similar to a drop of oil being spilt on the water surface. The lobworm settled on the gravel and I waited. Over five minutes had passed, yet my eel just lay buried in the gravel. I was beginning to think that the idea was just another brainstorm on my behalf and not worth pursuing. Then out of the blue the eel emerged, his head came completely off the bottom as if he was sniffing the water. Within a couple of minutes he was engulfing my lobworm.

Watching this display of feeding I can now understand why so many eels are deep hooked when fishing worms, maggots and small fish. The speed my lobworm went into the eel's mouth had to be seen to be believed.

As I watched the eel started to nose round the area where I had deposited my lobworm. It seemed that the worm's body juices were still present in the water. He could smell this so therefore was sniffing out more food. After a few seconds of nosing round he turned and swam back, diving head first into the gravel. I fetched another lobworm from my wormery and broke the tail off about two inches from the end. Once again I repeated the procedure of depositing my broken worm into the tank. The occurrence that followed next was unbelievable. Without any hesitation whatsoever he shot out of the gravel and made a beeline to the broken worm. Once again the lobworm was engulfed in seconds. At first I thought maybe my eel had seen the lobworm falling through the water to the bottom. I quickly repeated the procedure to another lobworm, this time depositing the lobworm from behind. Within seconds his head lifted off the bottom as before. He turned on himself and swam over to the spot where the lobworm lay and happily swallowed it. My idea had worked. The eel could find the bait a lot easier and faster when broken in two, allowing more body juices into the water, thus putting a larger scent trail down. The question was, would my findings work on the bankside?

One rod was fished with the normal lobworm set up, the other fished with a broken worm and to the book; my rod fished with the broken worm or worms produced more runs and fish than the normal set up. My findings and information were passed onto my angling companion, Gerry Rogers. He also then proceeded to try my new lobworm set up. It was not long before Gerry started to have more runs on the new rig. As with deadbait sections, the broken worms were more productive. My findings were tried on many types of stillwater, plus trials were made on our local rivers. On every occasion the broken worms produced more runs.

During the early years of my eeling, most, if not all, of my deadbaiting was fished using whole fish baits. As we know the eel finds its food 98% by its highly sensitive smelling mechanism. Some years ago I had a small eel in my aquarium at home. I found by studying his feeding habits that when I dropped a full deadbait, usually a minnow, into the tank, with only needle holes in the fish, the eel experienced a considerable amount of difficulty in finding my offering. On some occasions, the eel was only a few inches away from the minnow. I then tried cutting the minnow in half before depositing it into the tank and to my surprise the eel would travel from one end of the tank to the other and seize the minnow section, not hesitating for one second. The problem of locating his food was made easy.

It was then time to put my findings into practice on the lake-side and on my waters where deadbaits were productive. My halfbait section became very successful. In fact it outfished the full-baits. To prove to myself that my findings were totally founded and not just a one-off, I

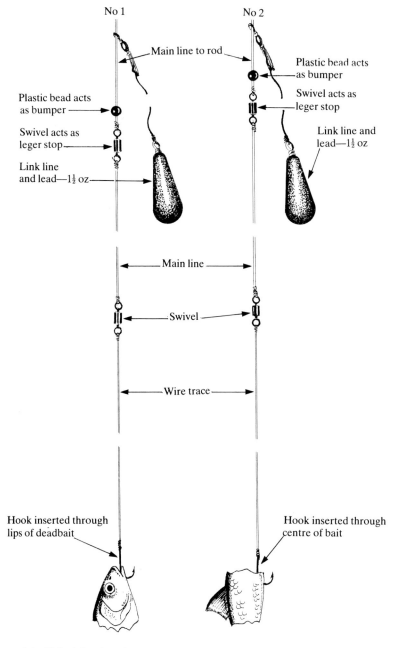

No 1

No 2

Main line to rod

Plastic bead acts
as bumper

Swivel acts as
leger stop

Plastic bead acts
as bumper

Swivel acts as
leger stop

Link line
and lead—1½ oz

Link line and
lead—1½ oz

Main line

Swivel

Wire trace

Hook inserted through
lips of deadbait

Hook inserted through
centre of bait

John Sidley's head section deadbait
hook set up (strike on first run)

John Sidley's middle section deadbait
hook set up (strike on first run)

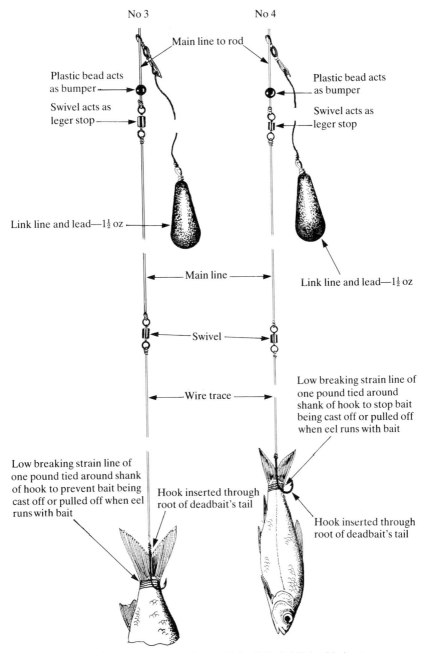

No 3

No 4

Main line to rod

Plastic bead acts as bumper

Plastic bead acts as bumper

Swivel acts as leger stop

Swivel acts as leger stop

Link line and lead—1½ oz

Main line

Link line and lead—1½ oz

Swivel

Wire trace

Low breaking strain line of one pound tied around shank of hook to stop bait being cast off or pulled off when eel runs with bait

Low breaking strain line of one pound tied around shank of hook to prevent bait being cast off or pulled off when eel runs with bait

Hook inserted through root of deadbait's tail

Hook inserted through root of deadbait's tail

John Sidley's ¾ or half section deadbait hook set up (strike on 2nd run)

John Sidley's full dead-bait set up (strike on 2nd run)

started to experiment with one rod set up with a full deadbait with needle holes punched in it (as in latter days), and a rig presented with my half section. I fished this two rig set up for over two months and the half bait rig outfished the full deadbait.

During the many months of feeding my eel in my tank at home, I came across more valuable information, which was to prove for me many more successful outings. Not only did my eel prefer sections of deadbaits to full ones, but the section more readily taken was the tail. On many occasions both halves of the minnow were dropped into the tank yet the eel would ignore the head and devour the tail. Once again I put my findings to the test. The tail section rig produced more runs. At first I could not put a reason to why this should happen. Mind you at the time I couldn't care less, as I was getting results.

One day while searching a local lake for fresh deadbaits which had died from natural causes, I noticed an abundance of fish that were dead in the margins, all having their heads severed. I put this occurrence down to rats. They had eaten the heads away first in the same manner that a domestic cat does, when given a fresh fish to eat. In time these dead fish would sink and fall to the bottom. Therefore it was more natural for an eel in search of food to find a fish in this way and consequently it accepted the fish without any fear.

Air injected baits for eels came into use when the angler found heavy weed growth or thick silt mud on the bottom of his venue. The problem was when the bait hit the bottom of the lake it would be covered in weed. This results in it being harder for the eel to find and the weed causes resistance on the main line. When using full fish baits, the swim bladder was left unpunctured and with the aid of a hypodermic syringe, air was injected into the bait.

When the bait was cast into the weed it would sink slowly and gently lie on top of the weed. If half sections of fish or strips of fish are used a small piece of cork or balsa wood is inserted onto the angler's hook rig. This again acts in the same way as the full air injected baits.

If a layer of soft sand or mud is found in your swim no real problem arises when using the above mentioned baits. However, the angler's link line connecting his lead should be made longer. This prevents the link swivel from becoming covered in silt. Again this covering of the link swivel will cause resistance. The problem this soft sand or mud causes the angler is when using any type of live bait such as lobworms, brandlings or maggots. In time these baits will start to bury themselves in the soft soil, thus covering themselves up. Using the hypodermic syringe, air can be put into these baits to suspend them just off the bottom.

One other method of presenting a bait over heavy weed growth so that the bait lies on the top, is to make a half-cocking leger. These types of legers can be bought or made by the angler. The shop bought ones are made from plastic, the bottoms weighted with lead. The plastic tops are buoyant so that the link line and bait are able to lie on top of the weed.

One type of bait that I have not gone into, but I think must be worth mentioning is 'livebait'. This type of eel fishing I have not researched in any great depth myself, but I know of anglers who have. The presentation of the livebait can be used either by legering, float fishing or even float paternostering. I feel myself that many problems would be involved in this type of eel fishing amongst which are:—

1. Where to present the hook without the eel feeling it.
2. How many hooks to involve in the rig.
3. When to strike.

The other problems are the false runs given by perch and, of course, pike.

Livebaits do take eels and have produced some monsters indeed. The 8 lb 8 oz British Record of 1922 taken by C. Mitchell from Bitterwell Lake fell to a float fished live roach while Mr. Mitchell was pike fishing, plus a good few more eels of eight pounds and under caught on livebaits.

If liphooked livebaits were used to help keep the bait alive, fished on either a float or leger rig but excluding very small livebaits under 2 oz, the second run will have to be awaited. Once again there is a chance of deep hooking or the eel feeling the hook and rejecting the bait. Incorporating a two hook rig, again the eel feels the wire or hooks and rejects the bait before a strike can be made. Failing that the eel can ignore the hooks and wire, swallow the complete rig and the end result turns out to be a dead eel. If the hook was placed in the livebait's tail, it would restrict its movement and swimming action, therefore it would just lie on the bottom.

If I were to go into this method of eel fishing myself, I would use a hook set-up which involved a hook being put into the livebait's dorsal fin. As most, if not all, eels seize a fish bait across its middle, an instant strike made wherever possible would, I think, give a better hooking chance. Apart from the problems arising in working out a most successful hooking rig, the amount of hooked pike or perch on some waters would be very high. All great stuff if you wish to put these types of fish into your landing net, but a nuisance if your true quest is eels.

The amount of pike and perch I have taken over the years using deadbaits for eels is quite staggering. Mind you, one pike I took on a tail section roach from Westwood in 1981 pushed my scales round to 23 lb 3 oz. That type of pike I don't mind and are welcome, but most are only small jacks and at night can give you one hell of a tussle trying to subdue.

Fishing livebaits on the surface or mid-water again will bring unwanted pike and perch. On many occasions I have seen pike feeding on the surface in the hours of darkness, feeding both in the margins and in the centre of a lake whilst I was boat fishing. I presume they were feeding on the small fry which come to the surface at night-time in their thousands. This could explain the reason why some eels are taken just under the surface, i.e. feeding on the fry.

As I have said I have yet to go into any detail myself on this method of eeling. I know of other eel lads who have. They confirm to me what I have said about the problems of setting up a reliable hook rig plus the problem of false runs given by pike and perch. Yet at the same time I think this method should be looked into a great deal more, for eels, when taken by livebaits, seem to be of a very large size. Maybe I am too old now to change my ways. Yet I think the new up-and-coming eel lads of today could come up with the right answer.

If you do come up with an answer and I am not too far gone in years, please give me a ring on: 021 777 9802.

Since the writing of the manuscript for the first edition of my book, I have gone into the method of sub-surface rigs, surface rigs and off-the-bottom bait rigs. I have now added to my book the successes I have had using these methods and of the rig I have made to present the baits. I have now also done a lot of eeling using the 'hair-rig'. This method, so-called, for the bait is attached to the hook by means of a short piece of light nylon, a rig developed by Kevin Maddocks and Lenny Middleton to overcome the problem of carp which have become shy of their lines.

My reasons for using this rig were not because of eels rejecting my bait because they could feel the hook or wire trace, it was to help me a great deal in preventing the deep hooking of eels on lakes where I found the head of eels to be the predatory type, i.e. large mouth, big head and teeth like a hacksaw blade. On these waters there was nothing neat about the run regardless of the baits used, they just screamed off like express trains, some of the eels not even stopping with the bait. If left to run, I'm sure they would have taken all of my 200 yards of line off the spool. A close friend of mine fished one of these types of waters after I told him about the eels we had using eel sections for bait. I forewarned him of the type of runs and the risk of deep hooking. Before dark my friend took a $1\frac{1}{2}$ pound eel on worms and to the book, the hook was way out of sight. To save wasting the eel, he removed the eel's head and lip hooked it onto his end rig. Now believe me, the head of a $1\frac{1}{2}$ pound predatory eel is one hell of a mouthful. Within two hours of casting the head out, a run developed. I'm not sure my friend knew what to do. Should he wait for the eel to stop and strike on the second run, or strike when the eel was on its first run? After a few seconds of the eel picking up his bait, he had no choice but to strike on its first run,

Gorge rigs

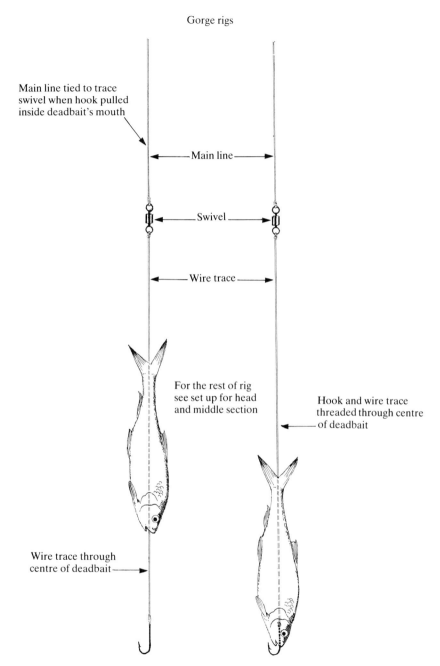

Main line tied to trace
swivel when hook pulled
inside deadbait's mouth

Main line

Swivel

Wire trace

For the rest of rig
see set up for head
and middle section

Hook and wire trace
threaded through centre
of deadbait

Wire trace through
centre of deadbait

Drawing showing how to pull
wire trace through deadbait
with the aid of a baiting needle

The gorge rig (strike on 2nd run)

Hair rigs

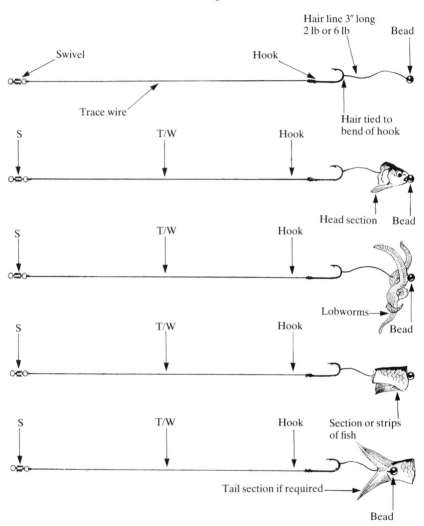

for this eel was not going to stop. The line on his reel was getting lower and lower. Bail closed, he wound down. He was greeted with a solid force and a rod bent nearly double. After the netting my friend was putting onto his scales an eel weighing in at 4 lb 8 oz and 1 lb 8 oz eel's head way out of sight. His 4 lb 8 oz eel was truly deep hooked.

After setting up my rig in the normal manner, I then got a length of nylon line with a breaking strain of 2 lb. This I found great when casting out small baits up to 40 yards, but when ranges of over 70 yards were called for, I then stepped up the breaking strain of the nylon to 6 lb. This prevented the hair from breaking off on a hard cast coupled to $1\frac{1}{2}$ oz leads.

With the aid of a baiting needle, I then threaded onto my hair the bait being used. To prevent the baits from slipping off the end of the hair rig, I tied on the end a small devon bead. The bait now put onto my rig, I tried the other end of my hair to the bend of my hook. The knot I used was the same as I used to tie my main line to my swivel. From the end of my bait on the hair to where it was tied onto the bend of my hook, measured about three inches. On the waters where I find the eels to swallow the bait fast, or experience many dropped runs, or the very finicky bites, the hair rig is put into use. It has accounted for many a lip-hooked eel and less dropped runs on waters where eels seem to be one step in front of the angler.

On some waters the hair rig does not work and many fish are missed. As yet I have not come up with the answer as to why this should happen. Yet on those waters where the hair fails, the standard leger rig is a winner. Maybe on these waters the eel has yet to wise up to the angler's bait presentation, but I believe it won't be long before they do. Never underestimate a big eel. They can be, and are, as crafty as any other big fish. They have to be, to grow that big.

(FOOTNOTE—The only fish bait where I have found it not necessary to use the hair rig is when using the tail section rig. With the hook set in the root of the tail, the second run has to be awaited. Deep hooking is cut down and dropped or finicky runs are not encountered. This applies to both types of eels found in your venue, i.e. big mouth or small mouthed eels.)

Please remember — litter loses fishing

Runs, Striking, Playing, Unhooking and Handling

The runs from eels, using all types of baits, can vary from one extreme to the other, regardless of the type of venue fished. Using worms, dead fish or specials, the first indication of a bite developing will be signalled by a sharp 'beep' tone of your bite indicator, providing you are using one. This will coincide with your visual indicator twitching up. Following this, your indicator will 'yo-yo' to your butt ring and your buzzer will sound off continuously as the eel takes free line.

If using worms, small sections of fish or specials, the rod should be picked up from its rests and two or three coils of line removed from the reel spool by hand, the bail arm then engaged. The main line is checked to ensure the bail arm roller has picked up the main line. If it is not checked and the strike is made with the main line only halfway round your bail, your bail arm will fly open and spare line given. After having pulled three coils of line from your reel, your accepting fish takes up all the slack line, which will be indicated by your visible indicator becoming tight on your main line and staying up by the butt ring. A strike should now be made.

The other type of run given by an eel is the one which is known to the specialist angler as a 'screamer'. This word means that the eel will be taking free line from your spool so fast that a visible indicator on your main line will stay at the top of your butt ring at all times during the eel's run, instead of dropping and rising as in the 'yo-yo' run. This fast type of run can cause the angler problems in trying to close the bail arm of his reel and checking to see if the main line is engaged round his roller. These runs are so fast that even giving spare line off your reel will serve no positive object. To overcome this problem, my method is to place my hand over the face of my reel spool then strike. My hand over the reel spool is in fact acting as my bail arm.

The last type of run encountered is the one we call the 'twitcher'. This run is indicated by your visible indicator moving an inch or two on your line, your buzzer making a broken 'buzz' sound, then stopping.

This procedure can happen a few times. The twitching is caused by the fish not swimming off with the bait. This type of twitch bite can result in a deep hooked fish, for the eel can so easily swallow the bait on the spot. To strike these type of runs, close the bail arm of your reel, slowly wind your indicator to a few inches under your rod butt and then as soon as another twitch is seen, strike. All the above mentioned runs, and how to strike, will one day have to be put into practice by you. All will become quite easy to perform with patience and practice.

The playing of eels, if one could call it that, is somewhat of a bullying action. The first job the angler should do before casting out is to make sure the clutch on his reel is set right. This should be done by pulling the main line off the spool whilst the bail is in the closed position. If the angler is using a main line with, say, a breaking strain of eleven pounds, the clutch should only be set so line will just slip free when a strike is made. Only enough line slip should be given on the strike to prevent a break. Do not fish with the clutch locked right down. The eel's main defence when hooked is to start swimming backwards. Its tail is always in search of underwater obstacles such as tree roots, weeds, old branches, etc. Once its tail becomes entangled in these obstructions you can guarantee a lost fish. Once the strike is made, the angler must wind strongly, removing the eel from the bottom of the stillwater or river. This done and the eel is off bottom, the pressure should be eased off, keeping the rod tip high and winding steadily and the eel will come to the waiting net with ease.

If one thinks hard about bullying the eel it will come as common sense that the more one keeps bullying, the more the eel will fight. It is the same as if I punched you, you would punch me back. In fact this steady winding seemed to confuse the eel. The only time any slack should be given to the eel is when the fish makes powerful downward surges with its tail. To overcome these powerful surges, the angler should lower the rod tip with each surge. This action will act like a shock absorber (similar to the elastic on a roach pole). This downward surge by the eel will be encountered more at the bankside when waiting to net the eel.

Most eels when hooked will start to swim backwards. In fact they can swim just as well going backwards as forwards. Another defence the eel has is to spin round like a spinning top. This action should not cause you too much concern as long as a swivel is used on the end rig. The angler should not be surprised when playing the eel to find his line go completely slack. Do not be fooled into thinking the eel has come off, instead wind as fast as you can and gain line quickly, for it is a certainty that your eel is swimming towards you, heading for an unseen obstacle like an undercut bank or tree roots. Do not be shocked either by the eel that leaves the water on its tail in the same way a salmon

A 6-7 January eel. Initially John was pike fishing but had dropped runs and mauled baits so switched to his J.S. eel rig baited with a sandeel head.

The five best of ten caught on worm at Kyer Pool, Tenbury Wells; a 5-07, three 4's and a 3 plus.

Margin fished worm resulted in this nice brace.

These 22 eels were taken off the surface over 20 feet of water. The best weighed 4-5 and were caught from the boat at Barnt Green Reservoir.

An opening night fish of 4 plus from Titley Lake near Leominster.

The 'T' shirt says it all – the best of a 16 fish catch of eels up to 4-14.

One night's work – 27 eels to 6 pounds.

The business end of a fish-eating specimen. Note thick lips, broad head and large mouth.

An eel angler's paradise – these two swims represent perfect lairs for big 'snakes'.

Another 4 pound plus eel from Kyer Pool.

Four good 'snakes' pose for the camera.

does. If this occurs, be ready to give slack by lowering the rod tip.

I believe that the worst part of subduing any eel is at the landing net. My procedure is to have my landing net submerged. I bring my eel over the net, making sure that at least half of the eel is in the net. This achieved, I make one powerful lift, and as I do my fish should drop into my net. If not and the eel slips out, then I am in real trouble for one does not get many chances at attempting the procedure again. When netted do not make the mistake of putting your landing net down close to the water. Do not forget that when playing a good sized eel, you could have well over $3\frac{1}{2}$ feet of fighting fury under the surface. One mistake made by you could mean the loss of a fish of a lifetime.

After landing and placing the eel onto the ground in a suitable place, if the hook should be found to be in the top jaw, gently push the hook inwards and in an upwards direction. If found to be in the lower jaw, vice-versa. If the hook is found to be in the corner of the mouth, again repeat the above. If the hook is in the corner but well back into the eel's mouth, care should be taken, for the point of the hook will be very close to the eel's eye socket. If this is the situation, I would not recommend trying to remove the hook by pulling it backwards through the hole. I would recommend the opposite. Push the point and barb of the hook out and with the aid of the wirecutter, snip the point and barb off the hook. The rest of the hook will then fall clear when pushed inwards.

Sadly, on occasions the hook will be found to have gone right through the eel's eye. A very upsetting sight (sorry) indeed. If this is the case, then again repeat the above mentioned. If the hook is found to be well down the eel's mouth, the aid of two forceps will be needed, one for opening the eel's mouth to the required distance. Please do not use any sort of pike gag. With the aid of the other forceps, push the bend of the hook very gently and in a downward direction. A couple of steady pushes should free the hook. If the hook should be found in the eel's throat and well back, extra care should be taken. In this area are located all the eel's life organs, i.e. heart, liver and so on. Abuse and heavy handed work will result in the eel's death.

The other position the hook will be found in, when deep in the eel's mouth, is on either side. If this is the case again take great care for the eel's gill rakers will be at risk. Once again repeat the above with the aid of two forceps. If removal is impossible I would advise you to cut the point and barb off. If these cannot be removed then cut the hook as close as you can to where it enters the eel's flesh. If the hook is out of sight then no attempt should be made to try and remove it. Once again repeating the same procedure as before with two forceps, cut the trace hook length as far down the eel's throat as possible and leave well alone.

If at any time during the unhooking of your eel the fish should start to pump blood out of its gill covers with every gasp, it would be best to dispatch the eels as humanely as possible. In addition if the eel's body starts to become discoloured, like blotches appearing in different areas, this too is a sign that the eel is dying.

The best way of dispatching the eel is to take a very sharp knife, and hold the eel at the back of its pectoral fins, which will be found near the gill covers. A dry rag will help also to achieve a better grip. With the knife, make one clear cut across its neck. This will sever the head in one movement. I must admit the unhooking of eels can be very difficult at times but if all the above mentioned ways of unhooking are put into practice, in time the angler will find the task to become more and more easy. The angler will also find that the larger the eel, the more easily you will find them to unhook. Time and practice will make perfect the job of unhooking.

The eel is very slippery to hold and because of the sheer muscle strength that they have in their bodies, some, if not all, anglers, at one time or another, experience great difficulties in trying to subdue their captive. Yet there are numerous ways the eel can be subdued without the angler having to jump on them or roll on the floor as if one was watching two wrestlers on the television. Small eels under one pound in weight will, and do, cause havoc, not only to the angler, but to the angler's end rig. They tie it in so many knots it would take Houdini to untie them. Subduing these small eels I'm afraid is up to you on the day. There is no real worthwhile method I could advise. The only thing I would remark on this problem is to have patience.

One method which was widely used years ago was the 'cross or groove method'. This method came from the old folk tales of Ireland. The cross was said to scare the devil out of the eel if laid on its back in one of the grooves made in the ground in the shape of a cross. The method does work very well. They lie quite still, enabling the angler to unhook them. It is known that if the eel was left for too long in this position it would die. The reason this happens as yet has never been fully explained, but I will put my own thoughts forward a little later on. When the angler has decided where to fish, he would then dig out a groove on top of the bank or near his swim. The groove should be deep enough only for the eel to be laid in so it cannot turn back onto its belly. The length of the groove should not exceed forty inches and width no more than three inches. Yet I must laugh to myself thinking of some of these grooves I have seen made. Some were so deep and long I think the angler concerned was thinking of lying a double figure conger eel into them.

Some grooves looked as if they had been dug out by a J.C.B., but one must stress that these larger grooves can be dangerous, for most were made along the footpath of the lake, canal or river. At night time an angler walking along the path unaware of these grooves could very easily lose his footing, causing a serious accident. The groove was also a dead give-away to a visiting angler new to the water. Find one of these grooves and you may well have found a productive eel swim.

I mentioned earlier on that if the eel was left on its back for a long period the end result would be death. I have put my own conclusions to why the eel so quickly dies. During the unhooking of an eel in the early hours of one morning, I laid an eel of 2 lb 12 oz onto its back. As the eel lay quite still on its back I went about the job of removing my hook from its lower jaw. As I was trying to remove the hook I heard a faint noise, a sound like when air is let out of a balloon while holding the mouth-piece straight. At first I was quite baffled as to where the sound was coming from. Then I noticed the eel's gill flaps puff out. This action by the eel is done solely to store oxygen in its mouth while out of the water. The eel can usually hold its gills in this inflated position for over ten minutes at a time but as I looked at the eel's gills inflate, they become deflated within a second and then the faint noise of air could be heard. I watched as the eel inflated its gills at least eight or nine times and on every occasion they became deflated. The eel could not store oxygen while in this upside down position. Turning the eel back to its natural position it inflated its gill flaps once more but this time they stayed inflated. The eel showed no signs of being unable to hold its gills inflated while in the upright position. This is why I believe the eel dies so quickly while on its back; it cannot take in oxygen.

Another way of holding the eel is to use newspaper. This method I found to be very messy and one which again could cause harm to the eel. The faults about this method was that newspaper became stuck to the angler rather than the fish. The second fault was that some anglers just left the newspaper behind on the bankside—you can imagine the mess. A real eyesore and one which could cause the banning of night time fishing or worse still ... the loss of a water. The third fault with newspaper was the amount of slime removed from the eel. This slime on the eel's body is a protective coating acting against any diseases.

A drug called 'MS-222' was used to knock the eel unconscious while unhooking or taking photographs. The drug is used by filling a large container full of water and adding so many drops per gallon of water used. The eel was then deposited into the container whereupon the drug would act. Another way of administering the drug is by using a hypodermic syringe. The syringe is filled with the right quantity of the drug then inserted under the eel's gill flaps. Great care must be taken while adopting both these methods. Instructions to the amount of drug given must be read very carefully, as if not, an overdose can be given. Even when the drug is given in the proper dose, before the eel can be returned to the water it must be completely nursed back to full health. If not and returned unstable, the eel could easily fall to any predators such as herons or pike.

Over the years I have tried all the above methods yet the one that I recommend is to lie your eel on a damp cloth, a wet keep-net or on any moss or grass. With both hands hold the eel down on its side and with one hand covering the eyes. Do not use force by holding the eel tight, the more pressure put onto the fish the more it will fight to get free. Very gently and with a damp hand, again to prevent slime from being removed, stroke the eel's body, starting from its head down to its tail. You will find that the eel will lie quite still, then very gently remove the hook. The most important thing to remember when holding or trying to subdue any sizable eel is to take your time. As I've said, the more pressure put onto the eel the more it will retaliate. At times I even talk to my eel while doing the above mentioned, saying things like 'come on my baby—I'm not going to hurt you'. I must admit you do get a few funny looks by any others present on the bankside, but I feel it gives me confidence and it does work.

Let us not forget that eels are many years old. My 7 lb 1 oz eel from Earlswood was said to be sixty-eight years old. If one starts ill-treating fish of that age the result will be a very dead fish. Statements made about eels being very hardy fish is all nonsense. No fish will stand for abuse, not even an eel. I know of eels that have just dropped dead in the angler's hands, although they were only lip-hooked and being treated with great care. One eel of over six pounds that died was sent away to a fish biologist. His report said that the eel had died of a heart attack. So remember, take your time in unhooking, handle with care and be as gentle as possible. You will then find your task of holding and unhooking made more easy.

One final point I should like to make: a practice I have seen used many times is the one when the eel is grasped behind the gill covers by hand. This area I must admit gives the angler a better grip, either for unhooking or when taking photographs, but I must stress that damage can be caused to the eel's breathing mechanism. At all times do your best to avoid these areas.

Prebaiting

If I were to spend many rod hours on one water and a venue that is very large and featureless, it would be then that I would choose to prebait my chosen swim. A few eel lads shy off using this method, putting forward the theory that the eels entering your swim could engulf all your free offerings, become full up with food and consequently ignore your hook bait. True, but I think this is the chance the angler has to take. Other anglers scorn this prebaiting saying that if the venue holds a large head of eels it will attract them from all over the venue, causing the angler a lot of aggravation, striking at small fish all night. Once again true, but at least I will know that my prebaiting programme is doing its job. If eels were not forthcoming to my rods, regardless of size, it would be then that I would start to worry. Let us be honest, we all have our share of the mediocre fish while searching out that elusive specimen. If my prebaiting attracts the small eels then it is only a matter of time before that big specimen finds my offerings.

On a water where the eel population is small, but the eels present very large, the prebaiting method is a 'killer'. I proved this when fishing a water in Northampton and a lake in the Midlands. At the time I was involved with a specimen group. There were six of us who fished these waters. Five of the lads could not be bothered to prebait their swims but I did. My fellow group members' results at the end of the season were nil. My total was six fish, the best at 8 lb 3 oz, the smallest at 1 lb 10 oz. As you can see a small eel was taken yet five others were large specimens. This water is in the Midlands and as yet I have never heard of an eel being taken from an unprebaited swim. A one-off venue maybe but if it can happen at one venue it could happen on another, maybe on the venue that you are fishing and finding it hard to get any runs—let alone any eels—and the talk in the local pub is 'there's no bloody eels in that venue!'—Think about it.

Before I started on my prebaiting campaign, the runs given by a taking eel were the usual couple of twitches, followed by a very fast run. Some runs were going so fast I was unable to close the bail arm of my reel. Yet after I have prebaited my swim the runs became slower.

In fact one could not readily call them eel runs. They were more like very slow bream bites, some bites giving the typical line bite, just raising my indicator a few inches then slowly dropping back. The eels entering my prebaited swim were not even moving off with my bait. This did cause a few problems for the angler had to be on the alert at all times. If not, a deep-hooked eel was the end result. A strike had to be made at the smallest possible movement of the indicator. My own explanation as to why the eels acted in this manner was they were feeding confidently. As most of our fishing is done at weekends and holidays, the eels were left undisturbed to feed for five days. Once they had found my prebaited swim they made regular trips back to the area to feed. I find that when there is sufficient food put into a swim, the fish tend to come and feed more confidently, picking up the bait and eating it on the spot, not belting off.

Eels and other coarse fish act the same way as ducks do on a pond. Throw in a couple of pieces of bread and a mad scramble follows, the end result being the duck rushing away from the brood to eat its prize. Yet on the other hand, throw in enough bread at once and the ducks will eat it on the spot, not running away—there is enough food for all.

These slow-type runs given by the eels will also happen where an area of the lake abounds in dead fish, due to the wind blowing them there. There again, these are prebaited swims—a prebaiting programme that nature is doing for you; an opportunity which should not be over-looked. Carp, tench and bream anglers nearly always prebait the area in which they are going to fish, hopefully to educate their quarry into taking their baits and to bring them into a certain swim chosen by the angler. So why not adopt the very same method into your eeling?

Worms, maggots, and dead fish used as prebaiting items will attract eels, yet at the same time these baits attract pike, tench, bream, carp, roach, perch and so on. All was O.K. if only the odd species of fish were present in the swim but if a large shoal came into my area, the chances of having a run from an eel was very remote, and if any pike came along the chances of an eel were nil. I find large eels specially to be loners, very rarely, if at all, swimming round with other shoal fish. The only times I have found a large gathering of eels is when the resident coarse fish begin their ritual of spawning. The eels will not be far away ready to reap up the harvest of fish eggs.

What I had to find now was a bait which would not attract other species of fish in any numbers, only eels. I then thought of the dead body I had seen pulled from the River Severn when I was a young lad. This corpse was full of small eels. At first I thought they had come from out of his clothing but at a later date, I was told his body was full of small eels. I also remember two dead sheep that I had seen pulled from the River Ouse near Northampton. The carcass of one of the sheep had

A 5 lb 13 oz consolation prize—an hour earlier a much larger fish bit through 18
pound B.S. Berkeley wire

two very large eels inside it when removed from the water by two farm
workers. I also thought of the tales the old water bailiff had told me
at Earlswood Lakes. When lobworms were in short supply due to a dry
spell, they would use the white strips of intestines out of a chicken. I
then decided to prebait with chicken offal plus a few other ingredients,
which I think would be best not mentioned. A month before the season
opened on June 16th, I deposited twenty pounds of the chicken offal
into my swim and my results were very rewarding. Only a handful of
other species of fish were taken from my swim. In most cases the runs
were from eels—it had worked.

I must stress that you must first gain permission. Firstly from the
owner or owners of the water concerned, for some are not too keen in
having a load of chicken offal thrown into their lake, and then secondly

Swimfeeder rig

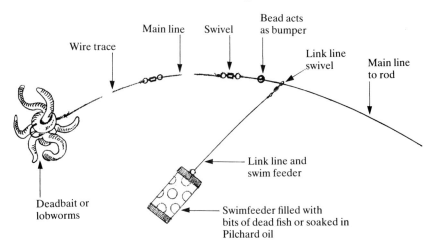

Wire trace
Main line   Swivel   Bead acts as bumper
Link line swivel
Main line to rod

Link line and swim feeder

Deadbait or lobworms

Swimfeeder filled with bits of dead fish or soaked in Pilchard oil

from your local Water Authority, to see if you can prebait with offal. Some byelaws prohibit the use of such ingredients. In prebaiting four venues with chicken offal and in different parts of the country, on all occasions my method has produced the goods both with small eels and some very large specimens. I'm not saying that prebaiting will bring record-breaking eels but it will make the difference between successful outings and the ones that keep producing blanks. You have nothing to lose so give it a try.

We all know that the eel feeds more by smell than sight or vibration, so in order to help the eel angler while fishing large featureless waters, or a swim which may only be fished once, for example, by an angler on holiday, the following may be useful. In my early years of prebaiting, the food used was either chopped up dead fish, worms or fish-based cat food—all good stuff to use. Later the use of attractors was brought into practice. In the same way sea anglers deposit 'rubby-dubby' into the sea to attract sharks, a rubby-dubby attractor is used for eels as well. This is made up from a hessian sack filled with chopped up dead fish and tied to a rope. The sack is then thrown into the angler's swim whereupon all the body juices of the dead fish are released into the water, hopefully to attract eels from far afield. The sack is either left in the swim all day or night and baited rods fished in the same area.

The only fault with this method was that a hooked eel could easily become entangled in the rope tied to the sack. If the sack was thrown in without a rope attached to retrieve it afterwards, it would not be long before the bed of the venue became littered with rubbish and the complaints from the other pleasure anglers fishing the water would cause,

I'm sure, a lot of aggravation indeed. A far more easy way of putting a scent down to the eel was developed in the form of the large blockend swimfeeders. These were filled with chopped up fish, smelly fish based cat food, sardines and even cotton wool soaked in pilchard oil, plus dried blood mixed with breadcrumbs or soil. All played the same role—to put a scent into the water.

The swimfeeder rig was used either with or without a hook attached. If no hook length was used on the swim feeder, it was cast out to the required area and rods fished with hook rigs around it. The eel would pick up the smell of the filled up feeder, come to inspect the source of smell and find the angler's baited hook—a most productive method as well. The other method used by the angler was to inject his baits, like fish, lobworms, brandlings, snails, slugs, maggots and so on, with an additive such as pilchard oil or any other liquid that could be injected into his baits with a hypodermic syringe and a liquid which would put a strong smell into the water. It did not always have to smell of fish, just as long as a smell could be released.

All the above methods were used by the angler on his holidays to a new water, someone fishing a swim only once, or by the angler who wished not to put food down to the eel. These methods were also used by the eel angler who liked to deposit food into his swim but was unable to, due to the distance required or the venue having no boats. The swim feeder caps could be removed, the feeder filled with food and the ends sealed either with ground bait or soil. The feeder then cast out, the angler could twitch the feeder back, resulting in the food being left where required as the soil or ground bait dissolves.

All the above mentioned have produced eels and good results to the anglers who have used them, myself included. On a water that I know to hold large specimens with plenty of cover, or a venue that is very large and featureless, I prefer to prebait my chosen swim. I have put my reasons forward and my results. I think you will find them well founded, regardless of what other eel anglers have said. On some waters, a prebaiting programme is a must.

Surface Rigs, Live and Deadbaits

In my previous book, I touched upon the subject of fishing for eels on the surface while fishing in depths of water over 20 feet and using as bait either live or dead fish. At that time in my eeling exploits, I felt I had not done enough of this type of eel fishing to write on the subject. I'm glad to report that I have now used the above methods and taken a good few eels. I would now like to put forward my methods and my findings on this new type of eeling.

The rig that I have been using for this type of eel fishing is more easily explained by looking at the drawing. You will see that with this rig the bait can be fished just off the bottom, mid-way or just under the surface, regardless of the depths found in your swim. I will now try my best to explain the setting up of this eel rig. With rod and reel all set up and your main line passed through the rings, I then place a one and a half ounce Arlesey bomb onto my main line. To the swivel of my Arlesey bomb I place a large split ring. This does away with the small swivel which is in the lead. The large split ring helps the line to run free if fishing over bottom weed or heavy silt mud, for to use a link line on your lead with this rig, the chances are very high in the line becoming entangled with your wire trace—end result—the float will not rise in the water, and if an eel was to take the bait from the bottom of the lake she would have to tow the whole rig with her. With that amount of resistance, a dropped bait will be the end result.

My next step is to make up my wire trace. This is 15 lb P.D.Q. wire at least 12 inches long. The extra length being obvious, the risk of a bite-off is great if a pike should come along and take your bait. A Mustad hook size to suit the size of bait is used. My deadbait hooks range from size four to a size two. These are whipped onto the trace. I then whip onto the other end a size 8 Berkley swivel. My hook trace is now ready. With an Arlesey bomb on the main line, I then place a large bead in front of my split ring. The bead acts as a bumper to the knot that I have tied to a swivel on the end of my line. To the other side of the swivel I tie a short length of my main line—say 6 inches long. At this point I add a short length of balsa wood, which is 4 inches long and half an inch wide. The ends are rounded off with a file and a hole drilled through the centre large enough to allow my main line to pass through. This will act as my float and allow me to fish any depth I wish. The float after being made is sealed with black or green paint, then given two or three coats of clear varnish. My line is passed through the centre of the float. I tie to this end the swivel which is connected to my wire trace. This done, the float is then locked onto my main line. The rig is then ready for use.

An Optonic buzzer, monkey climber indicator or even a drop-off back-bite alarm can be used with this rig. What must be used on this rig is a line clip, for if the baits are fished just off bottom or mid-water, the rig must be fished under tension. On the surface the line can be held on the reel spool by placing a small stone or coin. At all times the rig is fished with an open bail arm.

Livebaits, deadbaits or even lobworms placed onto the hook, the angler then casts the bait to the required spot. When the lead hits bottom the float and bait are wound back to the lead. This done, the angler then lets out free line from the reel. You will easily see how much line is being taken as the float lifts your bait from the bottom. This rig acts in the same way as a sunken float paternoster when pike fishing. The above done and the required depth decided upon, the line is then placed in the line clip. Your chosen indicator is then mounted onto your line.

I have been using livebaits, deadbaits, whole and in sections, plus bunches of lobworms on this rig. As other eel anglers have said, I have found nothing finicky about the runs when using this rig; believe me there is no mucking about. The eel belts off like an express train when the bait is seized. The really fast runs come along when the bait is being fished mid-water, or on the surface in depths of over 8 feet. I feel the eels are returning to the bed of the lake after seizing your bait. In my rig you will see that the eel has to tow the float along with her, as yet this has caused me no problems with dropped runs.

I now turn to the hooking of my fish baits. A lot of eel lads use the Vic Bellars type of hook as used in pike fishing. These are a big single hook with a small bait holding hook either whipped by wire to the shank of the large hook, or soldered to the shank. The small hook is placed into the bait and the large hook does the hooking of the eel. Myself, I'm not too keen on this type of method, my reasons being in case of deep hooking. With one hook in the gut the eel stands a fair chance of survival but with two, I fear deaths will be the end result.

As in bottom eeling, deep hooking does take place on the surface and mid-water rigs, regardless of bait being used, the only exception being on lobs. On livebaits, I have been hooking them in the root of the tail.

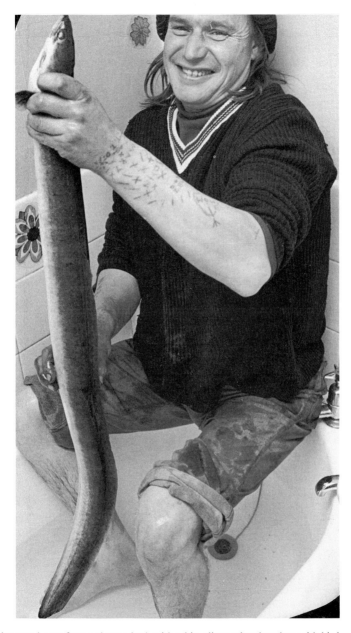

John says he prefers to share a bath with a big, slimy eel rather than with his better half!

They work well and seem to stay alive a lot longer than hooking them in the back by the dorsal fin, or through the lips. When a run develops, I await the second run. A strike made then, has indeed in most of my eels, resulted in the eel being lip hooked. The same applies when using tail sections. Once again as in normal legering, with tail mounted baits, a low breaking nod line can be used to help tie the bait onto the hook. This will prevent the bait being cast off or pulled from the hook when a fast run develops.

On head sections or pieces of fish, an instant strike is made. On the heads the hook is placed in the lips of the bait, and on pieces of fish in the centre of the bait. On lobs an instant strike is made also. As I have said, I am new to this type of eeling. I have tried it in the day and at night, with a moon out and with no moon and in all depths of water from only 3 feet deep up to 25 feet deep. On only one occasion did my rig produce all the runs while my bottom baits were untouched. As yet this type of eeling has not produced the monster snakes in any numbers. It produced eels yes, but one has only to look at the top 50 eel list to see where those big girls have come from—hard on the bottom to a standard leger rig. Clive Dennison, a first class eel angler and a member of the British Eel Anglers Club, has been using this type of eel fishing rig for a good few years. He has taken many eels while doing so. His best was 6 lb 4 oz, a great snake indeed. The depth of water Clive fished with his off-the-bottom, full deadbait rig was only 5 feet. The bait being fished was off bottom around 2 feet. To me any large eel could just lift its neck off bottom to seize the bait. This type of eeling we did many years ago without the need of floats. All we used was a deadbait with its swim bladder intact or injected with air. We found this rig to be very good when fishing over heavy weeds. All it did was to enable the eel to see the bait more easily. I will carry on using this type of rigs for my eeling, after all, it does produce eels, yet I feel it has a long way to go in beating the standard hard on the bottom eel rigs for that is where I believe those big old snakes spend most of their life and feeding hours. To finish my exploits on this type of eeling, it is worth noting that these rigs do not work on all waters. I have found the waters most productive using these rigs is where the head of the eel is of the predatory type, i.e., large head, mouth and an impressive set of teeth.

Obtaining Live and Deadbaits

As with making my wormery, I have had many phone calls from eel anglers, plus letters, asking me how I get my livebaits for eeling. The questions asked are: 'Do you go out with rod and line to catch your fish?' 'Do you have a supply of livebaits at home in tanks, as you do for pike fishing?' 'Do you use frozen fish baits?' The answer to all these is 'No'.

With all my eeling, regardless of the waters being fished, one or two rods are fished on lobworms, so when I arrive at my venue, at least I can get a bait out into the water as dusk starts to fall. After an hour into dark, I start netting the margins of the lake with my 42 inch landing net. After the first couple of sweeps, I have more than enough livebaits to take me through the night. This is done on every night I am at the water, or if I'm lucky enough to have to use all my livebaits in one night, I repeat the process. It's truly amazing the amount of small fish that come into the margins at night time and when darkness falls. One can see why the margins at night are a good bet for the eel angler to place a bait. The problem with carrying extra tackle to catch your livebaits is done away with and the expense of buying bait, nod hooks and the rest of your gear to start nod fishing. Also the need to have containers at home with a supply of live fish is done away with. In all the years I have been obtaining my livebaits in this way, I have yet to come across a water where my netting after dark does not work.

I do not agree with the use of frozen baits. I have tried frozen baits and fresh live baits despatched and used on the same fishing stint and at all times the fresh bait have out-fished the frozen ones. Deadfish which have been allowed to go off have been said to be very good due to the eels highly smelling out of food. I have tried this method and found it to be untrue. At times the 'off' baits never produced a run while the fresh bait has been going all night. Using my netting method, fish are killed as required, thus doing away with the killing of fish only to be thrown away at dawn if not used—to me a complete waste and a scene that will and can upset the pleasure angler who may be fishing by you. Those little fish may not mean anything to you, but a bait for an eel to another angler can be very upsetting. So on your next trip out, instead of carrying all that extra gear to catch your fish baits as darkness falls, get your landing net set up and do a couple of sweeps in the margins of your lake. Believe me you will have enough fish baits to last you all night long, and you must admit you can't get a bait any fresher. Simple ain't it! Also it prevents heart attacks from carrying a ton of fishing gear.

Margin Eel Fishing

Reading the chapter in my book on the location of eels, you will see that I mentioned the obvious hiding places, i.e. weedbeds, drop-offs, fallen trees, etc. areas where dead fish gather due to the prevailing wind, lock gates, etc., etc. You will also notice that my baits are all fished near a feature such as the above mentioned, but I feel an area which must be looked into more by the budding eel angler is the margins of your venue, for I feel that a lot of anglers are casting baits way out into the wide blue yonder. Remember eel fishing is not a casting competition. Putting baits out over 90 yards plus, unless covering, as I've said, a feature, all you are doing is fishing past where the eels will be feeding.

Walk round the margins of your venue during the day and you will see the food life available, either live or dead. If that does not convince you, then walk round your venue after dark and shine a torch light into the margins. The insect life and fish fry will be there in abundance, all easy pickings for an eel on the hunt for food. I can only name two of my eel waters where long range casting into featureless water has brought forth eels to me. All the rest have some sort of feature. Earlswood Lakes are a prime example. All my eels came from the margins of a weedbed, some of my big eels coming from only a couple of feet from the bank, and in depths of water only 10 inches deep. Once again do not be put off by how shallow the water is. If an eel can cover her back with water and the food is there, the eel will enter such areas. This has been proven to me time after time again with my pike fishing in the depths of winter, taking many pike, with fish over 20 lb in very shallow water. Once again the food was there, then why not the pike?

On some of my eel waters there are islands way out in the lake. From my fishing position, I have to pump a bait out well over 90 yards. The same applied with weedbeds. One could say I'm fishing long range, yes, but my baits are being fished once again in the margins. If I could sit out on the island, I would be fishing my baits in the same spot as if I had cast from the bank. The same with weedbeds, if fished from a boat; think about it. Fishing the margins on most of the venues will be a long waiting game, for the eels found in these areas are very few, but of a large size. As big eels feed on very small eels, the smaller eels will avoid these areas like the plague after dark. In most cases only one eel will fall to this type of fishing during the night stint, yet I always leave a bait in the margins after taking an eel just in case another eel overlaps the other eel's feeding area.

I have found the best times to fish the margins are the nights of no moon. Also when the night is very warm and humid. The water temperatures during the night holds longer in the margins, while a bait fished out in open water can be chilled off very quickly. This again can be proven by fishing out in the lake on a boat or on a stage. The air temperature will drop like a brick overnight, yet on the bank at the same time, with a little tree cover, you will find it over two overcoats warmer.

Extra care will be needed when fishing the margins, regardless of bait being used for the eels tend not to run with your bait, but engulf it on the spot, so deephooking is at a high risk. So at the smallest twitch of your indicator or beep of your buzzer, be ready to wind down fast and strike the hook home. Do not wait for the run to develop.

A few eel anglers advocate the use of light lines for eels. Fair comment in swims that are like a swimming pool, with no snags to worry about. However when fishing margins there are many hidden dangers, i.e., tree roots, waterlogged branches, large boulders and of course the human jungle of old bike frames, wheels of all descriptions—the junk thrown in by the people who don't care. In this terrain you will need a line of at least 11 lb breaking strain. Believe me, you won't be able to give one inch of line. So on your next trip out to your venue, forget about the casting competition. You're not there to impress your friends on how far you can chuck a one and a half ounce lead. You're there to catch eels. Stick a bait in those margins and believe me, that's what you will do. You will catch eels and you will impress your friends a lot more when that big snake takes the needle of your Avon scales round. It's a great feeling, believe me.

Top Ten Eel List as at May 1990

Are the eels getting bigger in this country, or is it that more anglers are showing a great deal more interest in the searching out, and the capturing of specimen eels—i.e. fish from five pounds and over? I feel myself that there have always been more big eels swimming about in our waterways than a lot of anglers have given credit for. With the formation of the National Anguilla Club, the British Eel Anglers Club and now the Eel Study Group, the eel is becoming as popular as carp, tench, pike or any other big fish species, an interest which I believe has long been overdue.

From 1922 when Mr. C. Mitchell took his record breaking eel of 8 lb 8 oz from Bitterwell Lake, it was not until 1948 that his record fish was equalled with another eel of 8 lb 8 oz taken by Mr. Ward from Fritton Decoy. It then took until 1969 for the record to fall again with a fish weighing in at 8 lb 10 oz, taken by Alan Dart from Hunstrete Lake, near Bristol. Going by the many years separating these record eels, it seems strange that the record weight of 8 lb plus should be broken at least three times in 1985 alone, and with eight eels over 6 lb, plus five fish over 7 lb, taken in 1985 at the present date, one can see that the monster eel of Stephen Terry's taken from Kingfisher Lake in Hampshire and weighing in at eleven pounds two ounces, could mean that the record could be taken at any time. I have listed what I believe to be the true top ten eels taken by rod and line in this country.

1.	S. Terry	11 lb 2 oz	Kingfisher Lake, Hants.	Worm	June 1978
2.	C. Price	9 lb 13 oz	Revesby Res. Lincs.	Deadbait	Feb 1984
3.	?	9 lb 7 oz	Somerset Lake	Boilie	Aug. 1985
4.	D. North	9 lb 2 oz	Lancs Lake	Maggot	Sep. 1985
5.	S. Dove	9 lb 2 oz	Chase Water	Boilie	1989
6.	R. Woolham	8 lb 13 oz	Wem Pit, Shropshire	L. Meat	1984
7.	A. Dart	8 lb 10 oz	Hunstrete Lake	Deadbait	Aug. 1969

8.	J. Harrison	8 lb 10 oz	Calf Heath Res.	Lobworm	July 1983
9.	C. Taylor	8 lb 9 oz	Wem Pit, Shropshire	L. Meat	June 1981
10.	C Mitchell	8 lb 8 oz	Bitterwell Lake	Livebait	Oct. 1922

Note: An eel weighing 9 lb 2 oz was reported taken from the River Severn at Diglis Weir by a young angler named Peter Dombie. After making enquiries into this capture, I was told by Peter's mother, that the report was in fact a hoax. The eel was in fact a conger taken by Peter from the coast whilst on holiday.

Conclusion

I hope that having read this book and of my numerous exploits over the years in search of *Anguilla anguilla*, I have helped you in some way to improve your eel catches, but more important of all, helped you to put that personal best eel onto the bank. Believe me, it has been a very hard and laborious task putting down on paper the full aspects of eel fishing.

I have attempted to put the full facts forward on eels and eel fishing without I hope, too much red tape. I could have so easily filled more pages by writing about the night a fox ran through all my rods while I was night fishing the dam wall at Westwood Park, or of the badger who came to visit me in my brolly camp one night at Patshull Park, and of the graceful kingfisher skipping across the venues I have fished, in the early hours of the morning—all interesting reading, I admit, and I for one hope none of the above ever changes for it is part of our fishing; true Nature in the wild. Yet sadly the above happenings do not help me catch eels so are excluded from my writings. My prime aim is to catch eels.

In my book I have attempted my utmost to help you, the reader, achieve those same targets. I have in my book given you a lot to ponder on, but it is a wise angler who enters this branch of our sport with an open mind. Do not be afraid to try new methods as I did by fishing sections of deadbaits and broken lobworms. I was brave enough to break away from the old rituals of fishing full deadbaits and full lobworms and week-old deadbaits. My efforts were rewarded with some outstanding eel catches. Success does not come easy in the pursuit of specimen eels. You must be prepared to put in that 100% effort. There are, believe me, no half measures. If you decide to fish with a group or club or with a fellow eel angler, then make sure that all involved are as dedicated as yourself. If not, the effort and time you have put in could go to waste. If you decided to go after specimen eels after reading my book I welcome you to what I feel is the hardest branch of our sort. I wish you all a very bent and slimy landing-net and may all your blanks be rods.

I would like to put on record my sincere thanks to Mrs. Ann Taylor

and Miss Gay Cuber who typed out this manuscript. I would also like
to thank my very good friend and angling companion, Mr Gerry Rogers.
In addition, a great vote of thanks to Beekay Publishers.

John Sidley
(The Eel Ferret)
May 1990

Eel Clubs and Useful Addresses

No book on eels and eel fishing would be complete without a mention of the three eel angling clubs that exist today. First is the National Anguilla Club, established in 1962. At present the club has a membership of 30. Up until November 1980 all members had to be over 18 but this policy has now ceased and the club is open to all as long as the applicants concerned show an interest in eels and in eel fishing. The subscription is £5.00. Further details and membership form from the current Membership Secretary, Kevin Huish (address follows).

The second of the eel clubs is the newly formed Eel Study Group, being formed in the early 1980's. The club has a limited membership of around 20 anglers and to join you should have a proven track record in the capture of specimen eels. Most members are invited to join by other members of the group so membership is limited. For further information contact Kevin Richmond or Clive Dennison (address follows).

Third and last of the eel clubs is the British Eel Angling Club. This was formed in 1980 by Mick Bowles, Gerry Rogers and myself. The club was formed out of the outstanding success of my 'Put Eels Back Alive' campaign started in 1975. The BEAC is open to all eel anglers regardless of experience and sex. Since 1980 the club has enjoyed the company of over 500 members and currently in 1989 the club has a membership of 149. The BEAC along with the NAC is also affiliated to the National Association of Specialist Anglers (NASA), and the ACA, the Anglers Co-operative Association.

The BEAC year runs from January 1st to December 31st. Subscriptions at the present time for under 16's is £5.00 per year plus £2.00 joining fee. For over 16's it is £10.00 per year plus £2.00 joining fee. Overseas, but not BFPO members, under 16 is £6.00 per year plus £2.00 joining fee and for overseas over 16 it is £12.00 per year plus £2.00 joining fee. For further information on the BEAC write to the membership secretary, Mr Mick Bowles enclosing a SAE (address follows).

Since the BEAC was formed from the 'Put Eels Back Campaign' it is therefore a rule since 1989 that no member of the BEAC shall deliberately kill eels for food or for the use of hook baits in the capture of other species.

Eel Angling Club Membership Secretaries

The National Anguilla Club: Kevin Huish, 44 Albany Street, Ferndale, Rhondda, Mid-Glamorgan. CF4 5L. Tel. 0443 757140.

The Eel Study Group: Kevin Richmond, 20 Landmead, Glastonbury, Somerset. BA6 9DB, or Clive Dennison, 60 Plumtree Road, Thorngumbald, nr. Hull, North Humberside.

The British Eel Anglers Club: Mick Bowles, 64 Granville Road, Gillingham, Kent. ME7 2PB.

(please remember to enclose a SAE for a prompt reply).

Tackle Dealers and Manufacturers for the Eel Angler

Peter Drennan, Leopold Street Works, Leopold Street, Oxford. OX4 1PJ.
Paul Boote, Penfynnon, Moylgrove, Cardigan, Dyfed. SA43 3BW.
Alan Bramley, Partridge of Redditch, Mount Pleasant, Redditch, Worcestershire. B97 4JE.
Barrie Welham, Leeda Tackle, 14 Cannon Street, Southampton. SO9 2RB.
Edward Morris, Taylor and Johnson Ltd., Broad Ground Road, Redditch, Worcs. B98 8YP.
Andy Barker, Unit 6, Omega Workshops, Parkside, Coventry, West Midlands. CV1 2WE.
K. M. Products (Maestro Boilies, K. M. Safety Sack & Weigh Sling), Withy Pool, Bedford Road, Henlow Camp, Beds. SG16 6EA.
Bob Frost Tackle, 23 Bath Street, Leamington Spa. CV31 3AE.
Shimano UK, Unit B2, Lakeside Technology Park, Phoenix Way, Swansea Enterprise Park, Llandsamlet, Swansea. SA7 9EH.
E. T. Products, 7 Riverside, Stanstead Abbotts, Herts.
The Tackle Shop, Trevor Moss, 42 Tooley Street, Gainsborough, Lincs.
Dave Plummer, Norwich Angling Centre, 476 Sprowston Road, Norwich, Norfolk.

Bob Morris Tackle, 1 Lincolnshire Terrace, Lane End, Darenth,
    Dartford, Kent. DA2 7JP.
Fosters Tackle, 266 Kings Road, Kingstanding, Birmingham.
Nigel Williams Tackle, New Hampton Road West, Wolverhampton.
Bob Church & Co. Ltd., 16 Lorne Road, Northampton. NN1 3RN.